P9-CKP-384

DATE DUE

NO 30 '92	MY 1 '97	NO 10	
JA 15 '93	MY 27 '97		
FE 19 '93	MY 29 '97	DE 16 '02	
AP 19 '93	OC 30 '97		
	DE 17 '97		
JE 10 '94	MY 2 '98		
JE 30 '94	NO 23 '98		
RENEW	NO 23 '98		
DE 2 '94	FE 22 '99		
NO 1 '95			
MY 5 '95	OV 21 '99		
JE 1 '95	OCT 2 '99		
OC 20 '95	DE 7 '99		
DE 15 '95	NO 14 '00		
DE 22 '95	MY 29 '01		
NO 8 '96			
NO 18 '97	FEB '01		

DEMCO 38-296

Arnold P. Goldstein

Research Press

2612 North Mattis Avenue
Champaign, Illinois 61821

Riverside Community College
Library
OCT '92   4800 Magnolia Avenue
Riverside, California 92506

HV
9069
G64
1990

Advisory Editor, Frederick H. Kanfer

Copyright © 1990 by Arnold P. Goldstein

94 93 92 91 90   1 2 3 4 5

All rights reserved. Printed in the United States of
America. No part of this book may be reproduced
by any means without the written permission of the
publisher. Excerpts may be printed in connection
with published reviews in periodicals without
express permission.

Copies of this book may be ordered from the
publisher at the address given on the title page.

Cover design by Cindy Carlson
Composition by Compositors Typesetters
Printed by McNaughton & Gunn

ISBN 0–87822–308–8
Library of Congress Catalog No. 89–69839

For Lenore

Days of kindred gone before,
Lives that speak and deeds that beckon.
One in name, in honor one,
Guard we well the crown they won.
What they dreamed be ours to do,
Hope their hopes and hope renew.

Our Celebration Song

Contents

Tables

Acknowledgments

This seven-state, 19-site project was brought to fruition by the combined energies of several juvenile facility administrators and a very talented group of 35 staff member interviewers. They have my sincerest appreciation for helping to transform this effort from idea to reality. Especially helpful were Larry DiStefano, Barry Glick, Linda Albrecht, Sue Yeres, and Tom Coultry. I enthusiastically thank you all.

This is a project in which, uncharacteristically perhaps for academics, we tried to talk little and listen a lot. The project's basic premise was that delinquent youths themselves, as a result of their life experiences, have much wisdom to share regarding the causes of juvenile delinquency, its prevention, and its remediation. So listen we did, and much of interest was our reward. As this book reveals, experts-by-experience do indeed have much to offer that is insightful, novel, utilitarian, and, not infrequently, wise. We are most grateful to the source of these valuable offerings, our 250 research-partner adjudicated delinquents.

Arnold P. Goldstein
Syracuse University

CHAPTER 1

Introduction

In recent decades, many hundreds of investigations and much speculation by criminologists, psychologists, sociologists, and others have posed, in one form or other, three interrelated questions: What causes juvenile delinquency? Which interventions effectively reduce it? and, How may it successfully be prevented? The fruits of this research and theorizing have been plentiful and varied. Physiological, psychological, sociological, sociopolitical, and—we believe, most consistent with the realities of juvenile delinquency—multidimensional perspectives have been advanced.

These several theories of causation, and their implications for intervention and prevention, are collectively what the professional experts believe about the immensely important phenomenon of delinquency. Much of value has been derived from these beliefs, in the form of better understanding of the roots of delinquency as well as a broad and varied spectrum of group, individual, community, diversionary, and other intervention techniques.

Yet juvenile delinquency continues in the United States at distressingly high levels, and recidivism rates point to only very modest success at best for the interventions that have been employed. Are there other types of experts whose views on delinquency causation, intervention, and prevention are of potential value in helping us understand more fully and accurately why youths become delinquent and how delinquent behavior can be reliably reduced and prevented? We believe that such expertise may exist, is largely untapped, and is very much worth pursuing. We refer not to yet another discipline of professional expert but, instead, to *experts-by-experience,* juvenile delinquents themselves.

DELINQUENTS AS EXPERTS

Does the experience of *being* delinquent convey expertise in *understanding* delinquency? We do not know, but we strongly believe so. Our justification for this position derives from several sources. First,

1

contemporary writing offers a number of insightful examples of drawing upon people who have "been there" to understand human behaviors other than delinquency. Some are vocational, such as Funke and Booth's (1961) *Actors Talk About Acting* and Pekkanen's (1988) *M.D., Doctors Talk About Themselves*. Some examples are in the mental health disciplines, such as Shapiro's (1962) "Patient Wisdom: An Anthology of Creative Insights in Psychotherapy," Strean's (1959) "The Use of the Patient as Consultant," and Yalom and Elkin's (1974) *Every Day Gets a Little Closer: A Twice-Told Therapy.* From Kitwood's (1980) *Disclosures to a Stranger: Adolescent Values in an Advanced Industrial Society*, we learn in depth about adolescent values regarding family, peers, work, and self, as described by (nondelinquent) adolescents themselves. Other examples focus on the experience of poverty, as in Williams and Kornblum's (1985) interview study of 900 teenagers, *Growing Up Poor;* on the experience of minority status, as in Meltzer's (1984) *The Black Americans: A History in Their Own Words;* or on both experiences, as in Monroe and Goldman's (1988) *Brothers: Black and Poor—A True Story of Courage and Survival* and Hanson, Beschner, Walters, and Bovelle's (1985) *Life With Heroin: Voices From the Inner City.* Other works present the experiential reports and resultant insights of adult felons. Among them are Irwin's (1970) *The Felon;* Abbott's (1981) *In the Belly of the Beast;* Manocchio and Dunn's (1970) *The Time Game: Two Views of a Prison;* Toruk's (1974) *Straight Talk From Prison: A Convict Reflects on Youth, Crime and Society;* and the Figgie International (1988) survey of almost 600 adult property offenders, *The Business of Crime: The Criminal Perspective.*

Closer still to the type of data base obtained in the present project, much of the basis for our belief in delinquents as experts on delinquency also derives from relevant interview studies of delinquent adolescents. Maher's (1966) and Adelson and Gallatin's (1983) investigations of delinquents' perceptions of the law are two such examples. Others are Shaw's (1930/1966) *The Jack-Roller: A Delinquent Boy's Own Story;* Strodtbeck, Short, and Kolegar's (1962) "The Analysis of Self-Descriptions by Members of Delinquent Gangs"; Roberts' (1987) *The Inner World of the Black Juvenile Delinquent;* Brown's (1983) *The Other Side of Delinquency,* and Bennett's (1981) *Oral History and Delinquency: The Rhetoric of Criminology.* There also exist several informative interview studies of unreported delinquent behavior (Gold, 1970; Kratcoski & Kratcoski, 1975; Kulik, Stein, & Sarbin, 1968; Short & Nye, 1957) as well as studies of experimenter-subject psychotherapy (Schwitzgebel & Kolb, 1964; Slack, 1960) using delinquents as paid experts on the topic of delinquency. Even more directly supportive of the purposes of our present project are the creative efforts of Mulvey and LaRosa (1986) and Shannon (1988), which have drawn upon the experience-based wisdom of ex-delinquents to examine criminal careers and the naturalistic occurrence of delinquency cessation. Together, these several interview-based research reports are certainly a strong beginning in support of our delinquents-as-experts position.

ORDINARY KNOWLEDGE AND LAY THEORIES

In spite of these useful and relevant beginnings, no study such as our present one has been conducted previously. We have undertaken this study because we believe the experience-based perspectives of delinquent youths can both cast a significant new light on the etiology of delinquency and serve as an heuristic source of utilitarian, intervention-relevant hypotheses. Many years ago, Lindblom and Cohen (1929) wrote promotively about the value of what they termed *ordinary knowledge* as a supplement to and, at times, even a replacement for *professional scientific knowledge*. As Lang (1988) more recently described it:

> Ordinary knowledge is drawn from experience,
> common sense, personal analysis and reflection,
> intuition and accumulated wisdom. . . . Ordinary
> knowledge is important because it renders complete
> the knowledge base that decision makers rely on
> when they are required to make a final determi-
> nation. (p. 21)

In his book *Lay Theories: Everyday Understanding of Problems in the Social Sciences,* Furnham (1988) takes an analogously supportive view of the potential value of such knowledge. He comments:

> Many of the social sciences, such as anthropology,
> criminology, psychology and sociology, have the
> unusual advantage of offering an *explicit,* formal,
> "scientific" explanation for certain behavioural
> phenomena (i.e., the causes of delinquency, poverty,
> alcoholism, etc.) while at the same time studying the
> layman's *implicit,* informal, "non-scientific" explan-
> ations for the same behaviours. . . . Despite the
> unique advantage to compare and contrast the
> structure, function and implications of these two

types of explanation or theory, these two research areas have . . . often developed independently of one another. (p. 1)

The present book is, at its heart, a book about ordinary knowledge and lay theories—the experientially derived wisdom of delinquent youths.

STUDY PLAN

Data Collection

To carry out the project's interviews, we enlisted the services of 35 staff members employed as teachers, counselors, or aides, or in other youth care capacities in juvenile residential facilities, group homes, or community aftercare agencies. A total of 19 sites located in seven states participated; all but two of the facilities were state owned and operated. The seven states included Florida, Michigan, New York, Ohio, South Dakota, West Virginia, and Wyoming. Via our own screening efforts and with the assistance of each site's administration, we sought as interviewers staff persons with interest in participating and a particularly strong record of developing good relationships with the youths in their facilities or agencies. Through on-site and/or mail-directed interviewer training, combined with quality assurance feedback and follow-up, the 35 participating interviewers were trained to conduct, with approximately seven youths each, individual, in-depth, semistructured interviews regarding the causes, prevention, and reduction of juvenile delinquency. (See the appendix for the project description and interviewer instructions used in contacts by mail.) In this manner, 250 interviews were obtained. Participating youths included both males and females; were White, Black, and Hispanic; and were mostly of lower socioeconomic status.

Interview style and content sought to blend relevance to the project's information-obtaining goals with the interview protocol flexibility necessary to obtain rich and individualized interviewee responses. We are in accord with Bogdan and Biklen's (1982) description of this strategy:

In keeping with the qualitative tradition of attempting to capture the subject's own words, and letting the analysis emerge, interview schedules . . . generally allow for open-ended responses and are

> flexible enough for the observer to note and collect
> data on unexpected dimensions of the topic. (p. 71)

Yet interviews cannot be too unstructured or unfocused, or relevant data will not be obtained. Thus, the general sense of our interview(s) for each participating youth may best be described as commencing in a topic-relevant but essentially nondirective, open-ended, and broadly structured manner and moving progressively—as directed by the richness or paucity of information being obtained—to a more specific, closed-ended, and narrowly structured interviewer style. As the flow of a given interview and the interviewer's sense of the quality of the relationship with the interviewee suggested, questions such as, Why do you think kids get in trouble? or, What's your opinion about why juvenile delinquency happens? or, What do you think can be done so that there would be less juvenile delinquency in America? at times yielded to questions of intermediate structure—for example, Do you think a guy's family or how he's brought up has anything to do with getting into crime? or, What about someone's friends? Does that have anything to do with getting into trouble? Then, if it seemed appropriate, the interviewer went on to such highly specific questions as, If someone's friends go straight or get in trouble, how does that affect a guy's own behavior? or, What if a father beats a kid a lot? What's the effect on the kid and whether he gets in trouble? In the large majority of interviews, such increasingly structured follow-on questioning proved unnecessary. Generally, interviewers opened with the broad-stroke question noted first and proceeded to follow the interviewee's leads in framing further inquiry.

We did not intentionally turn our planned interviews into journeys through youths' personal histories. That is, we did not inquire into the reasons they believed *they* had committed delinquent acts, the ways in which such behavior could have been prevented, or their personal or familial histories. However, our pilot interviews and more general experiences with delinquent youths strongly suggested that much of what participating youths would have to say would at times be personalized, revealing richly detailed events, experiences, and perceptions of both an historical and a contemporary nature that would be of considerable relevance to project goals. We welcomed such information. We did not press for it, and we respected each youth's right to keep the responses more or less depersonalized and about "the other guy." But when personal accounts were entered into, our questions gently, nonprobingly, followed the informational leads thus provided.

Our goal in making interview participation voluntary and anonymous, in selecting as interviewers the staff members with the best relationships with youths, and in orienting interview questions toward nonpersonal perceptions unless the youths chose otherwise was to make interview participation as pleasant, interesting, and noncoercive as possible. In the spirit of both Bogdan and Taylor's (1975) recommendation for high-quality unstructured interviewing and Slack's (1960) pioneering if rudimentary inquiry into the world of juvenile delinquency as delinquents see it, we sought in these several ways to have participating youths experience their project roles as *research partners* rather than as deviant objects of outside scrutiny.

To concretize this spirit, in addition to using the types of open-ended questions and gentle questioning styles that we have described, interviewers were trained to explain the nature of the research carefully, make clear the project's and the interviewer's intentions, assure anonymity, describe the specific procedures that constituted the research project (i.e., interview, transcription, analysis, write-up, dissemination), and pay continuing attention to building and maintaining an interviewer-interviewee relationship characterized by respect and trust.

Data Analysis

Typescripts of 250 interviews conducted with the participating youths constituted the project's raw data. Our broad data-analytic goal was to examine these materials in order to identify themes, classes of ideas, traditional and novel perceptions, and, more generally, the phenomenology of delinquency causation, prevention, and remediation as seen by delinquent youths themselves. Operationally, we employed the constant comparative method of qualitative analysis in seeking to accomplish these ends (B. G. Glaser, 1987; Hammersley & Atkinson, 1983; Schatzman & Strauss, 1973). Essentially, this method involved the careful reading and rereading of the interview transcripts; the simultaneous generating of coding categories based on both accepted behavioral science concepts and the ideas put forth by the youths themselves; the sorting of statements, perceptions, and themes into these categories; and the expansion, contraction, revision, and refinement of the coding categories as the coding process continued and the coder more fully discerned "the full range of types or continua of the category, its dimensions, the conditions under which it is pronounced or minimized, its major consequences, the relation of the category to other categories, and the other properties of the category" (B. G. Glaser, 1987, p. 221).

It is important to stress that, although we employed the coding and categorizing processes sketched in order to organize and summarize the mass of data constituted by 250 interview protocols, we have actively sought to maintain and reflect the richness of these data. We have attempted, as much as possible, both to report what *we* discerned the participating youths to believe and to share, in a verbatim manner, what *they* actually had to say. Our goal, in short, was both data-analytic rigor and phenomenological richness.

In pursuit of these complementary goals, the project investigator utilized both *conceptual levering* and *triangulation*. A conceptual lever is "any thinking device that both distances the analyst from his data and provides a new perspective on them" (Schatzman & Strauss, 1973, p. 118). Particularly useful in this regard are dual efforts to understand the interview data first through the eyes and concepts of one's professional discipline (i.e., *substantive levers*), and then from diverse perspectives (i.e., *logical levers*). As Schatzman and Strauss observe:

> To illustrate the utility of a substantive-logical lever
> combination: Imagine observing a city substantively
> through the eyes . . . of a realtor, an urban planner,
> and an urban historian; then vary the position of
> observation, logically, by walking along the streets,
> by bicycling and motoring through it and then flying
> above it in a helicopter. Assuming one were able to
> take these perspectives, in combination, the city as
> "data" would naturally present itself in a variety of
> conceptual patterns. (p. 121)

Triangulation (Hammersley & Atkinson, 1983) as a further means of augmenting the depth, clarity, and yield of the data analysis was operationalized in the project via the diverse but complementary disciplinary perspectives of the project investigator and his protocol-judging consultant. The former read and categorized all interview typescripts; the latter did so with a substantial overlapping protocol sample.

A qualitative, in-depth investigation of the perspectives of delinquent youths on delinquency causation and intervention has not been conducted before. It was our overriding belief that the project as planned, conducted, and analyzed would yield substantial information of both theoretical and, especially, applied value regarding the phenomenology of delinquency per se and its roots, its reduction, and its remediation.

CHAPTER 2

Causation:
Professional Perspectives

The roots of juvenile delinquency have been a target of considerable formal theorizing and informal speculation within several academic disciplines during the past century. Much of the early etiological thinking was constitutional-physiological in nature and emphasized purported anatomical differentiators of criminal and noncriminal individuals. Such offerings have since largely been relegated to the status of historical, scientific curiosities with little contemporary acceptance. Much the same seems to be the emerging destiny of one of the major early psychological perspectives on delinquency causation, the psychoanalytic. Psychoanalysis appears in general to be in broad eclipse, and so are its positions on the etiology of juvenile delinquency. A second early psychological perspective centering on such notions as moral insanity, psychopathy, and other distorted personality constellations lives on today, as we shall see later, in a considerably transformed and more data-based form.

Following these initial constitutional-physiological and psychological speculations, sociology became heavily invested in diverse efforts to identify the core sources of juvenile delinquency. These several theory formulation attempts, which effectively moved the study of delinquent behavior away from individual concerns and characteristics to the study of collective social forces, were concretized in a creative and diverse array of theoretical positions. Their central concepts included such notions as strain or frustration growing from the discrepancy experienced by youths between aspiration and opportunity, assimilation into subcultures promoting deviance, control deficiencies issuing from a failure of familial and social bonding, the effects of the delinquency labeling process, and the consequences of living poorly in a capitalist society. These sociological strain, cultural deviance, social control, labeling, and radical theories had an especially strong influence upon etiological thinking about juvenile delinquency for many years, especially during the 1960s, an era of heightened attention to many social problems in the United States.

Perhaps because such thinking bore at best only partial fruit, theories began to center once again on more individualistic concerns. Both physiology and psychology reentered the picture, but this time in far more sophisticated and data-based ways than characterized their earlier incarnations. Physiological theorizing, with its current biogenetic and neurohormonal foci, grew from well-conducted comparative field research on twins and adoptees and equally well-conducted laboratory studies of genetic abnormality, behavioral inhibition, and hormonal function and dysfunction. Psychology, with analogous experimental rigor, offered new insights regarding personality characteristics differentiating delinquent and nondelinquent youths, and social learning theory put forth valuable perspectives on the means by which the behaviors reflecting such characteristics were acquired, performed, and maintained.

Yet even these theoretical advances, for all their empirical support, appeared to many to yield but a partial picture. That they were important pieces of the puzzle seemed likely; that they were only pieces and not the full picture seemed certain. For this reason of incompleteness (i.e., that physiology, psychology, and sociology each yield only a discipline-driven perspective), integrative, multidisciplinary theoretical perspectives on delinquency causation have begun recently to emerge. Several such offerings have appeared, and although the specific ingredients of each differ from position to position, most are multilevel, multidisciplinary, and integrative in their contents. We strongly applaud this development in the belief that juvenile delinquency is complex, multiply determined behavior whose remediation is most likely to be advanced to the degree that both causative theories proposed and interventions offered are similarly complex and reflective of the multiply determined nature of the behavior we are seeking to understand and alter.

Several monocausal and multicausal etiological theories of juvenile delinquency have been offered, both historically and in modern eras. (See Table 4 on pp. 146–147 for an enumeration of these theories.) In this chapter, we will present and examine this diverse array of constitutional, psychological, sociological, biogenetic and neurohormonal, and integrative perspectives on juvenile delinquency, reporting their substance, evaluating their empirical support, and distilling what each has to teach us about the significant, enduring, and difficult-to-change behavior called juvenile delinquency.

CONSTITUTIONAL THEORIES

Both the tenor and substance of each theory of delinquency causation that we will examine reflect the temper of each theory's respective scientific, moral, and political times. The mid-1800s was an era of biological determinism, greatly influenced by Darwin's theory of evolution, which by 1870 had begun to leave its imprint not only on the biological sciences but on the social sciences as well. In 1911, Cesare Lombroso, an Italian physician, proposed that criminals were morally (by dint of their criminal behavior) and physically (by dint of the qualities to be enumerated) a more primitive form of human being. The specific anthropometric indices of criminality suggested by Lombroso included cranial asymmetries, large ears, sloping shoulders, short legs, flat feet, and numerous other facial and bodily characteristics. *Homo delinquens,* in psychological makeup, was held to be insensitive to pain, lazy, shameless, and tending toward cruel and impulsive behavior more adapted to earlier, prehistoric eras. Such physical and psychological qualities, Lombroso held, could aid not only in distinguishing criminals from noncriminals, but also in differentiating among types of criminals (e.g., sexual offenders purportedly had full lips; murderers, very sloping foreheads). Lombroso was cognizant of the manner in which social forces also contributed importantly to the occurrence of crime, but his clear emphasis was upon the physical atavism just exemplified. Lombrosian thinking eventually posited less a criminal-noncriminal dichotomy and more a criminaloid continuum, with

> people who were less atavistic than Mr. Hyde but
> more so than Dr. Jekyll. Criminaloids, unlike born
> criminals, were not doomed to commit crime; they
> had a criminal tendency that might or might not be
> triggered by their experiences. The biological
> disposition to commit crime could, in other words,
> range from irresistible to nonexistent, according to
> Lombroso. (Wilson & Hernnstein, 1985, pp. 73–74)

Though some evidence later emerged in support of the existence of criminal-noncriminal physiognomic differentiations (Kozeny, 1962; Thornton, 1939), and considerable historical and contemporary evidence has appeared for the criminaloid continuum notion of a biological predisposition toward criminality (Christiansen, 1977; Dalgaard & Kringlen, 1976; Rosenthal, 1970b; Trasler, 1987), the social Darwinist core of Lombrosian thinking has received little philosophical or empirical support and considerable methodological criticism (H. Ellis, 1914; Goring, 1913; Wilson & Hernnstein, 1985). Much the same negative result (Hoskins, 1941; Montagu, 1941) has emerged for early etiological notions of crime and delinquency resulting from endocrine gland disorders (Schlapp & Smith, 1928).

But if the notion that specific facial or bodily features or glandular dysfunction could distinguish criminals from noncriminals fell into early disrepute, this was not the case for somatotyping, the idea that one's general physique (rather than localized measurements) was a significant cause and/or correlate of criminality. In a series of investigations conducted in the 1940s, William Sheldon put forth and evaluated the proposition that body build correlates with temperament as well as overt behavioral tendencies. His somatotyping procedure yielded three categories of bodily physique: endomorphic, a build tending toward roundness; mesomorphic, a build tending toward muscularity; and ectomorphic, a build tending toward linearity. Sheldon's (1949) study of nude photographs of 200 incarcerated delinquent youths showed them to be strikingly mesomorphic—muscular, broad chested, large boned, low waisted. Several investigators, working in diverse settings and comparing matched delinquent and nondelinquent samples, have confirmed this finding, whether through photographs or direct bodily measurements (Cortes & Gatti, 1972; Epps & Parnell, 1952; Gibbens, 1963; Glueck & Glueck, 1950). Why should there be a relationship between physique and delinquency? Sheldon (1942) observed that mesomorphy was characteristic not only of delinquents, but also of salesmen, politicians, and certain other occupational groups. A number of studies have shown mesomorphy to be associated with what Sheldon called a *Dionysian temperament*— extroverted, expressive, domineering, highly active, and, in its more extreme form, impulsive and uninhibited in its seeking of self-gratification. As comparative personality trait studies discussed later in this chapter support, temperamental disposition appears to provide the "correlational glue" joining mesomorphic physique and delinquent behavior.

PSYCHOLOGICAL THEORIES

Psychoanalytic Theory

Freud (1961) spoke of criminal behavior as growing from a compulsive need for punishment and stemming from unconscious, incestuous oedipal wishes. Crimes were committed, in his view, in an effort by the perpetrator to be caught, punished, and thus cleansed of guilt. Alexander and Healy (1935) have stressed the criminal's inability to postpone gratification. Bowlby (1949) points to the role of maternal separation and parental rejection. Johnson and Szurek (1952) have sought to explain criminal behavior as a substitute means of obtaining love, nurturance, and attention, or as a result of permissive parents' seeking vicarious gratification of their own id impulses via their offsprings' illegal transgressions. A number of other psychoanalytic theorists have sought to distinguish delinquent subtypes as a function of their hypothesized etiology—for example, latent versus behavioral delinquency (Aichhorn, 1949), neurotic versus characterological delinquency (Glover, 1960), neurotic versus milieu delinquency (Levy, 1932), sociologic delinquency (A. M. Johnson, 1949), and Redl's (1945) fourfold categorization of (a) essentially healthy youths who commit delinquent acts in response to environmental stresses, (b) youths who commit delinquent acts in response to acute adolescent growth crises, (c) the neurotic delinquent, and (d) the "genius" delinquent who suffers from disturbances of impulse control/superego functioning. More generally, Binder (1987) suggests that

> the delinquent operates, like the infant, under the
> pleasure principle and can neither endure frustration
> nor postpone gratification. A poorly formed and
> ineffective superego, stemming from inadequate
> handling in infancy, cannot overcome the pleasure-
> seeking forces of the moment, and the result is
> truancy, sexual offenses, theft, and other delinquent
> acts. (p. 20)

A. M. Johnson's (1949, 1959) subsequent explorations of a superego lacuna in delinquent adolescents provide a similar etiological focus. Cohen (1958), Nietzel (1979), and others are correct in pointing critically to the tautological circularity inherent in this psychoanalytic position: "Aggressive or acquisitive acts are often explained by underlying aggressive or acquisitive impulses. The evidence for these impulses . . . turns out to be the aggressive or acquisitive act to be explained" (Nietzel, 1979, p. 78). Nevertheless, the explicit and implicit emphasis in each of these several psychoanalytic positions on the major role of early childhood and familial contributors to subsequent delinquency has proved quite accurate, as evidence examined later in this chapter will illustrate.

Personality Trait Theory

As did the diverse psychoanalytic perspectives on criminal and delinquent behavior, those promoting one or another explanation of
crime and delinquency based upon the personality of the perpetrator essentially place the etiological source of such behavior exclu-
sively within the delinquent youth. In comparison to nondelin-
quents, delinquent youths are, we are told, more assertive, resentful,
suspicious, narcissistic, ambivalent toward authority, impulsive, and
extroverted (Glueck & Glueck, 1950); less submissive, anxious, cooperative, dependent, conventional, and compulsive (Glueck & Glueck,
1950); more egocentric, interpersonally disruptive, and unfriendly
(Conger & Miller, 1966); less shy, worried, or timid (Taylor & Watt,
1977); more deficient in attachment to social norms, alienated, or
unproductively hyperactive (Megargee & Bohn, 1979); more sensa-
tion seeking and externally controlled (Quay, 1965); and poorer in
sociomoral reasoning, interpersonal problem solving, role taking,
and empathy (Arbuthnot & Gordon, 1987).

Early interpretations of such purported personality differentia-
tion data were strongly negative:

> Several reviews have found little or no support for an
> association between personality and criminal behavior.
> Metfessel and Lovell (1942) concluded that sex and
> age were the only constants and that no clear-cut
> picture of a criminal personality could be drawn.
> Similarly, Schuessler and Cressey (1950) reviewed
> twenty-five years of research on thirty different
> personality tests. They concluded ". . . the evidence
> favors the view that personality traits are distributed
> in the criminal population in about the same
> proportion as in the general population." (Feldman,
> 1977, p. 140)

Part of this critique sought to explain the several personality differentiators previously noted as differences not between criminals
and noncriminals per se but, instead, as artifactual differences associated with socioeconomic status, intelligence, cultural background,
and, because most such research was conducted on incarcerated
prisoners, institutionalization itself (Hindelang, 1972; Wilson &
Hernnstein, 1985). When appropriate matching procedures were
used to control for such influences, over 80 percent of the studies
showed significant personality differences between groups of crimi-

nals and noncriminals (Tennenbaum, 1977; Waldo & Dinitz, 1967). In part on the basis of these data, a number of delinquency causation theories emphasizing one or another personality dimension or cluster of dimensions have emerged. These theories include extroversion, neuroticism, and psychoticism (Eysenck, 1977); psychopathy (Cleckley, 1964; McCord & McCord, 1964; Quay, 1965); moral reasoning (Arbuthnot & Gordon, 1987; Jennings, Kilkenny, & Kohlberg, 1983; Laufer & Day, 1983); conceptual level (Hunt, 1972); irresponsible thinking (Yochelson & Samenow, 1976); and rational choicefulness (Cook, 1980). Although clearly providing less than the total etiological picture, such personality causation thinking—as will be seen in our later examination of integrative, multicomponent theories—is an important contribution to a comprehensive understanding of the roots of juvenile delinquency.

Social Learning Theory

Psychology's major contribution to an understanding of the origins of juvenile delinquency has been its focus on the learning process—both the learning of offending behavior and the learning of prosocial alternative behavior. Bandura's (1973) social learning interpretation of aggression, Feldman's (1977) social learning analysis of criminal behavior, and Patterson's (1982) seminal work on coercive learning processes in families that are frequently criminologic are three of the especially noteworthy offerings in this context. The strong emphasis on the learning process central to these perspectives reflects the recent major shift in psychology away from unobservable, purported inner determinants of behavior—such as the superego-ego-id construct of psychoanalytic theory or the type and trait notions central to the personality theories just cited—toward external, observable influences upon overt behavior. We will examine these contributions later in this chapter, in our discussion of integrative, multicomponent theories, because several focus in part on the social learning process.

SOCIOLOGICAL THEORIES

Strain Theory

The discrepancy between economic aspiration and opportunity lies at the heart of strain theory, as do such discrepancy-induced reactions as frustration, deprivation, and discontent. Strain theoretical notions first appeared in Merton's (1938) article "Social Structure and Anomie," in which he observed:

> It is only when a system of cultural values extols, virtually above all else, certain common symbols of success for the population at large, while its social structure rigorously restricts or completely eliminates access to approved modes of acquiring these symbols for a considerable part of the same population, that antisocial behavior ensues on a considerable scale. (p. 673)

Cohen's (1955) reactance theory and Cloward and Ohlin's (1960) differential opportunity theory are both elaborations of strain theory. Each seeks to enhance that theory's explanatory power, especially with regard to delinquent behavior among low-income youths. Yet such an association between social class and delinquency is inconsistent (Linden, 1978; Rutter & Giller, 1983). Furthermore, though their economic status often remains unchanged, most low-income delinquent youths eventually become law-abiding adults. Hirschi (1969) also marshals evidence indicating that many delinquent youths do not experience the sense of deprivation-induced motivation central to strain theory, and R. E. Johnson (1979) suggests that strain theory holds little explanatory relevance for delinquent acts committed by middle-class youths. These and related caveats notwithstanding, strain theory appropriately survives to this day, its more contemporary versions seeking to be responsive to both changed socioeconomic forces (Simon & Gagnon, 1976) and evidence indicating that middle-class youths are just as likely as those from low-income environments to aspire beyond their means (Elliott & Voss, 1974). The theory survives not as an all-encompassing explanation of juvenile delinquency but as one component of integrative theoretical views on delinquency that consider it to be complex behavior derived from a complex of causes.

Subcultural Theory

Subcultural or cultural deviance theory holds that delinquent behavior grows from conformity to the prevailing social norms experienced by youths in their particular subcultural groups, norms largely at variance with those held by society at large and including, according to Cohen (1955), gratuitous hostility, group autonomy, intolerance of restraint, short-run hedonism, the seeking of recognition via antisocial behavior, lack of interest in planning for long-term goals, and related behavioral preferences. Miller (1958) describes these subcultural norms or *focal concerns* as centering around trouble, toughness, (out)smartness, excitement, fate, and autonomy. In this view, the adolescent is "drawn or socialized into law violation in an attempt to live up to the perceived expectations of his or her deviant associates" (R. E. Johnson, 1979, p. 2). Sutherland's (Sutherland, 1937; Sutherland & Cressey, 1974) differential association theory, Miller's (1958) notion of lower class culture as a generating milieu for gang delinquency, differential identification theory (D. Glaser, 1956), cultural conflict theory (Shaw & McKay, 1942), illicit means theory (Shaw & McKay, 1942) and what might be termed situational determinism theory (Clarke, 1977) are the major concretizations of subcultural theory. Of these, differential association theory has clearly been most influential. Delinquent behavior, according to this view, is learned behavior. Further, correctly anticipating evidence that had yet to appear, Sutherland held that the manner in which such behavior is learned involves processes no different from the ways in which any other social behavior is acquired.

A substantial diversity of findings lends considerable credence to the likely role of such association-engendered learning in the etiology of delinquency. Most delinquent acts are committed by youths in the company of others (Farrington, Gundry, & West, 1975). Youngsters attending a school or living in a neighborhood with high rates of delinquency are more likely to commit delinquent acts than are similar youths attending schools or living in areas with low rates of delinquency (Rutter & Giller, 1983). Males who admit to having delinquent friends are more likely also to admit to delinquent acts than are those who deny having such friends (R. E. Johnson, 1979; Voss, 1963). A youth's likelihood of committing a specific type of delinquent act is significantly correlated with the likelihood of commission of the same act by members of the peer group (Reiss & Rhodes, 1964), and the number of delinquent acts committed by a boy's friends are predictive of his own future convictions (West & Farrington, 1977). Self-report data indicate that, across alternative etiological bases for delinquency (delinquent associates, delinquent values, attachment to school, school performance, parental love, attachment to parents, occupational expectations, perceived risk of apprehension), the strongest covariate by far is delinquent associates (R. E. Johnson, 1979). Sutherland and Cressey (1974) have criticized differential association theory for omitting consideration of personality traits. Nettler (1974) has noted its disregard for situational determinants of criminal behavior. Nietzel (1979) asserts that the theory reflects an overly simplified view of the learning process, and Wilson and Hernnstein (1985) observe that it provides no explanation for individual differences and hence fails to account for the fact that within a given neighborhood, for example, some youths adopt deviant values and others adopt more conventional ones. Thus, as with aspiration-opportunity induced strain, it is appropriate to view subcultural influences as but part of the etiological picture—in this instance, however, an especially important part.

Control Theory

Although both strain and subcultural theories seek to explain why some youngsters commit delinquent acts, control theory operationalizes its concern with the etiology of delinquency by positing reasons why some youngsters do not. Everyone, it is assumed, has a predisposition to commit delinquent acts, and this theory concerns itself with how individuals learn not to offend. The central construct of control theory, the major mediator of such learning not to offend, is the social bond (Hirschi, 1969). Social bonds grow both from direct social controls (e.g., externally imposed restrictions and punishments) and from internal controls (resulting primarily from affectional identification with one's parents). Social bonds find overt expression, it is held, in attachment to other people, commitment to organized society, involvement in conventional activities, and belief in a common value system. Hirschi proposes, for example, that "the prospects of delinquent behavior decline as the adolescent is controlled by such bonds as affective ties to parents, success in school, involvement in school activities, high occupational and educational aspirations, and belief in the moral validity of conventional norms" (quoted in R. E. Johnson, 1979, p. 2).

The weaker the social bonding, thus defined, the greater the purported likelihood of delinquent behavior. Both Hirschi (1969) and Elliott, Ageton, and Canter (1979) have reported evidence in support of this control theory hypothesis. Control theory and its variations (Hewitt, 1970; Matza, 1964; Nye, 1958; Reckless, 1961; Sykes & Matza, 1957) find particular support in the substantial empirical literature convincingly demonstrating the broad and deep influence of family factors upon the likelihood of delinquent behavior. Some of these factors are parental criminality (Osborn & West, 1979; Robins, West, & Herjanic, 1975); parental social difficulties such as excessive drinking, frequent unemployment, and the like (Robins & Lewis, 1966); poor parental supervision and monitoring (Patterson, 1982; Wilson, 1980); poor discipline practices—excessive, erratic, or harsh (Deur & Parke, 1970; Sawin & Parks, 1979; Snyder & Patterson, 1987); and, as compared to parents of nondelinquent youths, greater parental reward for deviant behavior, greater likelihood of becoming involved in coercive interchanges, more frequent modeling of aggressive behavior, and the provision of less support and affection (Bandura, 1973; Patterson, 1982; Snyder, 1977). Families of delinquent youths also often display a lack of shared leisure time (Gold, 1963; West & Farrington, 1977), intimate parent-child communication (Hirschi, 1969), and parental warmth (McCord & McCord, 1959; Rutter, 1971). In addition, parental reports suggest lack of attachment to the children and poor identification with the role of parent (Patterson, 1982). The central role of family processes in the social bonding sequence and its consequences for other domains of potential bonding are captured well by Snyder and Patterson (1987):

> Inept family socialization practices like poor discipline result in high frequencies of relatively trivial antisocial behavior by the child, like noncompliance, fighting, temper tantrums, petty theft, and lying. These inept practices may also result in poor interpersonal and work skills. Given that the child is antisocial and lacks skills, he is likely to move into the second stage of antisocial training. He is placed at risk for rejection by peers and adults, and for academic and work failure.... The rejected child is also likely to associate with other unskilled, coercive children, thereby increasing his opportunities to acquire, perform, and hone antisocial behavior.... As the child continues to develop in a family environment with poor socialization practices and to associate with deviant peers, his performance of antisocial behavior becomes increasingly frequent, varied, serious, and successful. (p. 219)

The drift neutralization control theory perspective was put forth by Sykes and Matza (1957). Delinquents, this position asserts,

> hold attitudes and values similar to those of law-abiding citizens. However, they learn techniques that enable them to neutralize those values and attitudes temporarily and drift back and forth between legitimate and delinquent behavior....

Neutralization theory assumes that delinquency
occurs when youths learn to disregard the controlling
influences of social rules and values. (Siegel & Senna,
1988, p. 169)

The particular rationalizations purported by Sykes and Matza to be
used by delinquent youths to operationalize this neutralization process include denial of responsibility, denial of injury, denial of a victim, condemnation of the condemners, and appeal to higher loyalty.

Reckless's (1961) containment theory is a third expression of the
control theory viewpoint. This approach holds that whether or not a
youth engages in delinquent behavior is a result of, on the one hand,
internal (e.g., restlessness, hostility, rebellion) and external (e.g.,
poverty, unemployment, relative deprivation) pushes, and, on the
other, inner (e.g., ego strength, good self-concept, high frustration
tolerance) and outer (e.g., sense of belonging, consistent moral
front) containment. As Siegel and Senna (1988) note,

Containment theory suggests that inner and outer
containments act as a defense against a person's
potential deviation from the legal and social norms
and work to insulate a youth from the pressures and
pulls of crimogenic influences. (p. 174)

Labeling Theory

In 1938, Tannenbaum described an escalating process of stigmatization or labeling that, he asserted, can occur between young delinquents and the communities of which they are a part. Minor transgressions are met with admonitions, chastisements, and perhaps
initial exposure to the police and court components of the criminal
justice system. As the transgressive behavior escalates, community
response hardens into a demand for suppression:

There is a gradual shift from the definition of the
specific acts as evil to a definition of the individual as
evil, and that all his acts come to be looked upon
with suspicion. . . . From the individual's point of view
there has taken place a similar change. He has gone
slowly from a sense of grievance and injustice, of
being unduly mistreated and punished, to a
recognition that the definition of him as a human
being is different from that of other boys in his

neighborhood, his school, street, community. The young delinquent becomes bad because he is defined as bad.

The process of making the criminal, therefore, is a process of tagging, defining, identifying, segregating, describing, emphasizing, making conscious and self-conscious. The person becomes the thing he is described as being. (Tannenbaum, 1938, pp. 87–88)

Mead's (1934) ea[...] :pt derives in large part from how [...] rt of labeling theory. Becker (1963 [...])75), Lemert (1967), and Schur (19 [...] n as it applies to diverse behaviors— [...] —that society at large labels as devia[...] elinquent be-havior (primary devian [...] explain, but delinquent acts subseq [...] : to the initial act(s) (secondary devian [...] "Persons are pushed to accept and e [...] expectations which are very difficu [...] imately, con-form to the stereotype [...] :m" (p. 111). Once the labeling pro [...] and Skinner (1987) note, conventi[...] labeled indi-vidual may be less likel [...] to engage in such behaviors may di [...] increasingly with other persons so [...] labeling the-ory fails to attempt any causative explanation of prelabeling delinquent acts (primary deviance) and too completely externalizes responsibility for the types of delinquent behavior it does seek to explain, it nevertheless quite appropriately sensitizes us to the likely substantial role of the stigmatizing process in encouraging the very behavior society wishes to reduce. The decriminalization and diversion programs examined in chapter 4 are positive responses by America's criminal justice system to this heightened awareness.

Riverside Community College District

Moreno Valley • Norco • Riverside

pg.13 - Cause

20- occur.

21- Becomes bad,... Becomes thing described

AA/EEO EMPLOYER
(909)222-8435

Radical Theory

Radical theory, sometimes termed the *new criminology* by its proponents (Abadinsky, 1979; Meier, 1976), is a sociopolitical perspective on crime and delinquency. Its focus is the political meanings and motivations underlying society's definitions of crime and its control. In this view, crime is a phenomenon largely created by those who possess wealth and power in the United States. America's laws, it is held, are the laws of the ruling elite, used to subjugate the poor, minorities, and the powerless. The specific propositions that constitute radical theory (Quinney, 1974) concretize its sociopolitical thrust:

1. American society is based on an advanced capitalist economy.

2. The state is organized to serve the interests of the dominant economic class, the capitalist ruling class.

3. Criminal law is an instrument of the state and the ruling class, which use it to maintain and perpetuate the existing social and economic order.

4. Crime control in capitalist society is accomplished through a variety of institutions and agencies established and administered by a government elite, representing ruling class interests, for the purpose of establishing domestic order.

5. The contradictions of advanced capitalism require that the subordinate classes remain oppressed by whatever means necessary, especially through the coercion and violence of the legal system.

6. Only with the collapse of capitalist society and the creation of a new society based on socialist principles will there be a solution to the crime problem.

As can be seen, radical theory goes far beyond mere matters of social labeling, differential opportunity, or like concerns. Its target is no less than the social and economic structure of American society. Although its preferred solutions appear to have little likelihood of becoming reality, radical theory has rendered a not unimportant consciousness-raising service resulting in increased awareness within the criminal justice system—and perhaps in society at large—of the degree to which social conflict, racism, exploitation, and related social ills are relevant to the etiology and remediation of criminal behavior.

BIOGENETIC AND NEUROHORMONAL THEORIES

The suggestion of a substantial genetic contribution to criminal and delinquent behavior dates back to at least 1916, in Goddard's "pedigree analysis" study of the so-called Kallikak family. Goddard proposed that feeblemindedness was inheritable and was associated 50 percent of the time with eventual criminality. Dugdale's (1942) subsequent examination of the genealogy of the Jukes family yielded rather similar conclusions. As Nietzel (1979) correctly observes, however, the genealogical method suffers from a number of limitations, especially the frequently poor reliability of birth and court records and the great difficulty of achieving "an unambiguous untangling of what it is exactly that the family transmits: genetic predisposition, psychosocial characteristics, or both" (p. 71).

A second approach to examining the possibility that criminal behavior grows in part from a genetic base, the comparative study of identical versus fraternal twins, has proven more adequate. Rather than relying on often inadequate records, conjecture, and deductive reasoning, twin studies compare the concordance rate for criminality (the percentage of twins sharing the characteristic) for monozygotic twins, who are genetically identical, and for dizygotic twins, who are only as genetically similar as siblings of either sex born at different times. If the monozygotic concordance rate is significantly higher, one may appropriately conclude that the given behavior is indeed genetically influenced. This is precisely the conclusion that has in fact been drawn in response to an extended series of such twin comparisons over the past 60 years. In the first such study, Lange (1928) found 30 prisoners in a Bavarian prison who were twins—13 apparently monozygotic and 17 dizygotic. Of the 13 monozygotic prisoners, 10 had twins who had also been in prison, as opposed to only 2 of the twins of the 17 dizygotic prisoners. Legras (cited by Rosenthal, 1970a), Krantz (1936), Christiansen (1977), and Dalgaard and Kringlen (1976) report similar findings, "presenting apparently impressive evidence of genetic transmission of the propensity to break the law" (Trasler, 1987, p. 187). It must also be noted, however, that over the decades during which these several comparative studies were conducted, as tests for zygosity became more reliable and recorded evidence of criminality more accurate, the criminality rate differences for the two types of twins became less pronounced. Furthermore, some investigators have speculated that pairs of monozygotic twins may be reared in social and even physical environments that are more similar than are the analogous environments of dizygotic twins. Consistent with the multiple causation perspective toward which the present chapter is leading, Trasler (1987) has responded to these several concordance studies by noting the likely interface of genetic transmission effects with companion social influences on criminality:

> The basic lesson to be drawn from twin studies seems
> to be that the intergenerational mechanism which

predisposes some [monozygotic] twin pairs to high
concordance for officially recorded delinquency is
probably mediated by both genetic transmission and
by social processes of bonding and interdependence.
There is no known way in which the respective
influences of inherited characteristics and learned
social patterns can be disentangled. (p. 189)

Another biogenetic research strategy is the adoption or cross-fostering study. In Denmark, where most of the research of this type has been conducted, adoptions and foster family arrangements are commonly made within a few days or weeks of birth, resulting in the child's having minimal contact with the biological parents. In these investigations, comparison is made of the criminality and delinquency of adopted or foster family offspring of biological parents having and lacking criminal records with offspring of analogously criminal and noncriminal adoptive parents (Bohman, Cloninger, Sigvardsson, & vonKnorring, 1982; Crowe, 1975; Mednick, 1977; Pollock, Mednick, & Gabrielli, 1983). These investigations, even more convincingly than the twin studies, provide evidence that the potential for criminality, especially persistent or recidivistic criminality, is influenced by the individual's biological inheritance. The degree of influence—"major" according to Trasler (1987, p. 190), "very small" in the view of Nietzel (1979, p. 75)—and the specific physiological and/or psychological means by which the influence occurs (Rosenthal, 1970b) largely remain to be clarified.

A final biogenetic avenue of research into the etiology of delinquency and criminality, cytogenetic studies, has proven much less fruitful. After a flurry of considerable interest, it now appears likely that chromosomal abnormality in the form of supernumerary chromosomes, perhaps associated with certain intellectually subnormal populations, is not to be found disproportionately among incarcerated delinquent youths (Wegmann & Smith, 1963; Witkin et al., 1976).

Neurohormonal theories of juvenile delinquency, though apparently not yet widely incorporated into current etiological theorizing, seem quite promising and are thus included here. L. Ellis (1987) notes that three seemingly disparate neurological views of delinquency have been put forth in recent years. The first, arousal theory, asserts that persons who are most likely to engage in criminal behavior appear to have nervous systems that are, in a sense, well insulated from the environment. They are more difficult to condition, more likely to endure pain, and more prone to seek high levels of stimulation. Further, Ellis notes, evidence suggests that such persons, when threatened, are unusually slow to shift from low or average arousal levels to a state of high arousal and slow to return to low or average levels when the threat has passed. The second, seizuring theory, notes that epilepsy is disproportionately present in the criminal, versus the general, population and that brain seizures may often be provoked by conditions of stress or alcohol consumption. On the basis of such findings, Mark and Erwin (1970) and Monroe (1970) have each speculated about seizuring as a possible cause of criminal behavior, especially regarding so-called crimes of passion. The third, hemispheric functioning theory, suggests that the manner in which the two cortical hemispheres functionally relate may dispose certain persons toward criminality. This perspective is responsive to evidence of right hemispheric involvement in the processing of emotional information (especially such so-called negative emotions as jealousy, hate, and cynicism), to the fact that the same hemisphere tends to control movement on the left side of the body, and to the several studies reporting that left-handed males are disproportionately represented in delinquent and criminal groups as compared to the general population. In his neurohormonal theory of delinquency, Ellis (1987) proposes that these three neurological perspectives each appear to describe effects of exposing the nervous system to high levels of androgens, especially testosterone. He marshals evidence suggesting that androgen exposure affects brain function by lowering overall responsiveness to arousal, by increasing the probability of seizures, and by causing cortical functioning to shift to the right hemisphere. The relevance of these findings to the etiology of delinquency lies in the association of the pubertal surge in testosterone with the rise in the incidence of delinquency associated with chronological age. Ellis thus asserts that "androgen infiltration of the nervous system . . . after puberty is likely to alter brain function in ways that increase the probability of delinquency and criminal behavior" (p. 509).

MULTICOMPONENT THEORIES

If this chapter were a competition for the "etiological truth" vis-à-vis juvenile delinquency, we would have to assert that each of the several theories we have examined has scored a partial victory, yet none is the winner. Juvenile delinquency is many behaviors, diversely motivated and expressed, apparently reflective of a very broad array of physiological, hormonal, personality, socioeconomic, familial, societal, and other roots. Any monocausal theory of its (their!) origin is destined to be incomplete. With very few (mostly historical) exceptions, however, each provides a partial truth; each contributes at least to some extent toward enhancing our understanding of the etiology of juvenile delinquency. This understanding, and our resultant ability to better predict and control delinquent behaviors, will thus be further advanced if we cease thinking in a monocausal, one-true-light, theory-A-versus-theory-B manner and move toward a more comprehensive theoretical posture in which the more potent monocausal theories are combined, in a rational and multimodal manner, to yield heuristic multicomponent theories. Several such theories have been proposed; they are the focus of the present section.

Differential Opportunity Theory

Cloward and Ohlin's (1960) differential opportunity theory seeks to combine the subcultural learning emphasis at the center of Sutherland's (1937, 1947) theory of differential association with Merton's (1957) concept of anomie consequent to sustained and substantial discrepancies between one's aspirations and opportunities. Cloward and Ohlin describe three overlapping types of delinquent subcultures:

1. Criminal, in which youths are committed primarily to crimes of theft, extortion and other illegal means of obtaining money. This subculture contains many adult models of such criminal behavior.

2. Conflict, characterized by frequent use of violence to obtain status and gain a reputation for toughness.

3. Retreatist, a largely detached, drug-oriented subcultural pattern.

Delinquent behavior, it is held, flows from these subcultural influences (especially the criminal) as they combine with numerous economic and cultural barriers to fulfilling legitimate aspirations. Although Nettler (1974), Nietzel (1979), and others have accurately pointed to the weaknesses of differential opportunity theory—poor operationalization of its major constructs, incorrectness of its assumption that delinquent and nondelinquent youths share common initial educational aspirations, and its focus on crime as primarily a lower class activity—it nevertheless is an explanatory step beyond the strain and subcultural theories taken singly.

Social Learning Theory

Social learning theory (Bandura, 1969, 1986) is a combined situational, cognitive, and physiological orientation to the acquisition of behavior. Although it has appropriately been utilized to examine the learning of many types of behavior, one of its major applications has been to the acquisition, instigation, and maintenance of antisocial behavior, especially overt aggression (Bandura, 1973; Feldman, 1977).

Table 1 is a summary statement of the processes that, according to social learning theory, are responsible for the individual's acquisition or original learning of aggressive behaviors, the instigation of overt acts of aggression at any given point in time, and the maintenance of such behaviors (Bandura, 1973).

Acquisition

Social learning theory, reflecting its aspiration to comprehensiveness, acknowledges that an unknown and perhaps substantial contribution to a given individual's potential to behave aggressively stems from neurophysiological characteristics. Genetics, hormones, the central nervous system, and the individual's resultant physical characteristics, it is held, influence his or her capacity or potential for aggression. Given the neurophysiological capacity to acquire and retain aggression in the behavioral repertoire, Bandura (1969, 1973) suggests that such acquisition proceeds by means of either direct or vicarious experiences. In both instances, the role of reinforcement looms large. Reinforcement of overtly aggressive acts, occurring in the context of trial-and-error behavior or under instructional control of others, is likely to increase the probability that the individual will learn or acquire aggression. Bandura speaks of reinforced practice as a particularly consequential event in the learning of aggression via direct experiences—be it childhood pushing and shoving, adolescent fighting, or adult military combat.

But social learning theory places heaviest emphasis upon vicarious processes for the acquisition of aggression. Such observational learning is held to emanate from three types of modeling influences—familial, subcultural, and symbolic. The physically abused person who, as a child, strikes out at peers and who, as an adult, batters his or her own child may be seen as having acquired such behav-

TABLE 1 Social Learning Theory: Processes Underlying Aggressive Behavior

ACQUISITION	INSTIGATION	MAINTENANCE
Neurophysiological characteristics Genetics Hormones Central nervous system involvement (e.g., hypo-thalamus, limbic system) Physical factors **Observational learning** Family influences (e.g., abuse) Subcultural influences (e.g., delinquency) Symbolic modeling (e.g., television) **Direct experience** Combat Reinforced practice	**Aversive events** Frustration Adverse reductions in rein-forcement Relative deprivation Unjustified hardships Verbal threats and insults Physical assaults **Modeling influences** Disinhibitory-reduced restraints Response facilitation effects Emotional arousal Stimulus-enhancing effects (attentional) **Incentive inducements** Instrumental aggression Anticipated consequences **Instructional control** **Environmental control** Crowding Ambient temperature Noise Pollution Traffic congestion Other characteristics of the physical, sensory, psychological environment	**Direct external reinforcement** Tangible (e.g., money, tokens) Social (e.g., status, approval) Alleviation of aversiveness Expressions of injury **Vicarious reinforcement** Observed reward (receipt-facilitation effect) Observed punishment (escape-disinhibitory effect) **Self-reinforcement** **Neutralization of self-punishment** Moral justification Palliative comparison Euphemistic labeling Displacement of responsibility Diffusion of responsibility Dehumanization of victims Attribution of blame to victims Misrepresentation of consequences Graduated desensitization

iors in part via observation of the abusive examples enacted by his or her own parents. Subcultural modeling influences on the acquisition of aggression are often exemplified by the behavior of adolescents in response to their observation of peer aggression or the behavior of new soldiers successfully indoctrinated into combative behaviors. And vicarious symbolic modeling on television, in the movies, and in comic books is also apparently a major source for the learning of aggression in the United States. Crucial here is the fact that such aggression usually "works." The aggressive model, be it parent, peer, or television character, is very often reinforced for behaving aggressively. Central to the observational learning process is the fact that individuals tend to acquire those behaviors that they observe others enacting and being rewarded for.

Instigation

Once the individual has learned how to aggress (and learned when, where, with whom, etc.), what determines whether he or she will in fact do so? According to social learning theory, the actual performance of aggressive behaviors is determined by the following factors.

Aversive events. Aversive events may occur and serve to evoke aggression. Frustration is one such aversive instigator. Adverse reductions in reinforcement are a second purported type of aversive instigation to aggression. Many commentators on collective aggression have pointed to this differential-opportunity type of instigation—especially in the form of a perceived sense of deprivation relative to others or of hardship perceived as unjustified, rather than deprivation or hardship in an absolute sense—as a major source of mob violence, riots, and the like. Verbal insults and physical assaults are additional, particularly potent aversive instigators to aggression. Toch (1969) has shown that, at least among chronically assaultive persons, the types of insults most likely to evoke physically assaultive behavior include threats to reputation and manly status and public humiliation. Physical assault as an aversive instigation to reciprocal behavior is most likely to occur when avoidance is difficult and the level of instigating assaultiveness is both high level and frequent.

Modeling influences. Just as modeling influences serve as a major means by which new patterns of aggression are acquired, so too can they function as significant instigators to overt aggressive behavior. If we observe another person—the model—behaving aggressively and not being punished, the observation can have a disinhibitory effect. If the model not only goes unpunished but is rewarded by approval or by tangible means for the displayed aggression, a response facilitation effect may occur. The model's behavior, in this instance, functions as an external inducement to engage in matching or similar behavior. The sheer sight of others behaving aggressively may function to instigate similar behavior in yet another way. Viewing such behavior often engenders emotional arousal in the observer, and considerable empirical evidence exists that arousal facilitates aggressive behavior, especially in persons for whom such a response is well practiced and readily available in their behavioral repertoire. Finally, Bandura (1978) also notes that modeling may influence the likelihood of aggression through its stimulus-enhancing effects. The observer's attention, for example, may be directed by the model's behavior to particular implements and how they may be (aggressively) utilized.

Incentive inducements. Feshbach (1970) and others have drawn a distinction between angry aggression and instrumental aggression. The goal of the former is to hurt another individual; the latter is an aggressive effort to obtain tangible or intangible rewards possessed by or otherwise at the disposal of the other. Incentive inducements to aggression relate to this second definition. As Bandura (1978) comments, "A great deal of human aggression . . . is prompted by anticipated positive consequences. Here the instigator is the pull of expected reward rather than the push of painful treatment" (p. 46).

Instructional control. Individuals may aggress against others because they are told to do so; such subcultural instigation to aggression is common in a gang delinquency context. Furthermore, obedience is taught and differentially rewarded by family and school during childhood and adolescence, and by many social institutions during adulthood (e.g., at work, in military service, etc.). Again, to quote Bandura (1973):

> Given that people will obey orders, legitimate authorities can successfully command aggression from others, especially if the actions are presented as justified and necessary and the enforcing agents possess strong coercive power. Indeed, as Snow (1961) has perceptively observed, "When you think of the long and gloomy history of man, you will find more hideous crimes committed in the name of obedience than have been committed in the name of rebellion." (p. 175)

Environmental control. The empirical examination of an array of external events as instigators to aggression has become a substantial investigative focus. Crowding, ambient temperature, noise, pollution, traffic congestion, and several other characteristics of the physical, sensory, and psychological environment have been studied for their possible instigative potency. Evidence reveals that each may (but does not necessarily) function as an instigation to aggression. Whether aggressive behavior does, in fact, grow from crowded conditions, hot days and nights, high noise levels, or the like appears to be a somewhat complicated function of the physical intensity of these environmental qualities, their perception and interpretation, the levels of emotional arousal they engender, their interaction, external constraints, and several other considerations.

Maintenance

Whether aggressive behavior persists, disappears, or reappears is largely a matter of reinforcement. When aggression pays, it will tend to persist; when it goes unrewarded, it will tend to extinguish. This simple and traditional S-R notion as applied to aggression becomes a bit more complex in social learning theory, as the number and types of reinforcements held to influence the maintenance of aggression become elaborated.

Direct external reinforcement. The persistence of aggressive behavior is directly influenced by the extrinsic rewards it elicits. Such rewards may be tangible (e.g., objects, money, tokens) or social (e.g., status, approval, recognition). They may take the form of the alleviation of aversive treatment (e.g., reduction of pain or other negative reinforcement) or, possibly, expressions of pain by the person against whom one is aggressing. These several classes of external reinforcement have been shown to have a maximal effect on the maintenance of aggression as a function of the same principles of reinforcement influencing any other behavior: latency, magnitude, quality, intermittency, and so forth.

Vicarious reinforcement. Vicarious processes, central to the acquisition and instigation of aggression, are no less important in its maintenance. Observed consequences influence behavior in a manner quite similar to the effects of direct external reinforcement. The aggression-maintaining effects of observing others rewarded for aggressing come about, Bandura (1978) suggests, via (a) the informational function—that is, the event tells the observer what aggressive acts are likely to be rewarded under what circumstances; (b) the motivational function—that is, the observer is encouraged by the observations to believe that similar aggressiveness will yield similar rewards; and (c) the disinhibitory effect—that is, the observer sees others escaping punishment for their aggressive behavior.

Self-reinforcement. Social learning theory proposes that there are also self-produced consequences by which individuals reward or punish, and hence regulate, their own behaviors. With regard to aggression, most persons in the course of socialization learn by example or rules that aggressive behavior should be negatively sanctioned, and they impose sanctions on themselves by what they say, do, or feel about themselves following their own aggressive behavior. Contrariwise, there are also persons whose own criteria for dispensing self-reinforcement are such that overt aggression is a highly rewardable source of pride. They are prone to combativeness and derive an enhanced feeling of self-worth from indulging in aggression successfully.

Neutralization of self-punishment. A number of other self-originated processes are suggested in social learning theory as factors that often function to maintain aggressive behavior. These primarily involve neutralization of self-punishment. They may take the several forms listed in Table 1, each of which is a cognitive effort on the part of the aggressor to justify, excuse, or ignore a behavior, or to avoid self-condemnation for aggression and its consequences.

Social learning theory has been the target of extensive empirical evaluation and, as reflected in the attention we have devoted to it here, has received considerable investigative support. Its current centrality in psychological theorizing is clearly justified. It is a multicomponent perspective immensely useful in its own right and, as we will show, also as a component in yet other multicomponent theories of juvenile delinquency.

Differential Association–Differential Reinforcement Theory

Burgess and Akers (Akers, 1985; Burgess & Akers, 1966) have creatively combined and integrated major aspects of Sutherland's (1937, 1947) differential association perspective and social learning theory's (Bandura, 1969) focal concern with the role of reinforcement. Differential association–differential reinforcement theory is operationalized in the following principles:

1. Deviant behavior is learned according to the principles of operant conditioning.

2. Deviant behavior is learned both in nonsocial situations that are reinforcing or discriminating and through that social interaction in which the behavior of others is reinforcing or discriminating for such behavior.

3. The principal part of the learning of deviant behavior occurs in those groups that comprise or control the individual's major source of reinforcements.

4. The learning of deviant behavior, including specific techniques, attitudes, and avoidance procedures, is a function of the effective and available reinforcers and the existing reinforcement contingencies.

5. The specific class of behavior learned and the frequency of its occurrence are a function of the effective and available reinforcers and the deviant or nondeviant direction of the norms, rules, and definitions that in the past have accompanied the reinforcement.

6. The probability that a person will commit deviant behavior is increased in the presence of normative statements, definitions, and verbalizations that, in the process of differential reinforcement of such behavior over conforming behavior, have acquired discriminative value.

7. The strength of deviant behavior is a direct function of the amount, frequency, and probability of its reinforcement. The modalities of association with deviant patterns are important insofar as they affect the source, amount, and scheduling of reinforcement.

Akers (1985) comments:

> The theory may be summarized as follows: Social behavior is learned by conditioning . . . in which behavior is shaped by the stimuli that follow or are consequences of the behavior and by imitation . . . of others' behavior. Behavior is strengthened by reward . . . and avoidance of punishment . . . or weakened . . . by aversive stimuli . . . and lack of reward. . . . Whether deviant or conforming behavior persists depends on the past and present rewards and punishments and on the rewards and punishments attached to alternative behavior—differential reinforcement. (p. 57)

The principal behavioral effects come from interaction in or under the influence of those groups with which one is in differential association and which control sources and patterns of reinforcement, provide normative definitions, and expose one to behavioral models. The most important of these are primary groups such as peers and friendship groups and the family. (p. 58)

Social Developmental Theory

Control and social learning approaches are the components of social developmental theory. Hawkins and Weis (1985) observe:

Delinquent behavior is likely to be a . . . result of experiences from birth through adolescence . . . early experiences in the family are likely to influence social bonding to the family . . . as well as the likelihood that social bonds of attachment to school and commitment to education will develop. . . . The social influence of peers becomes salient during adolescence itself. If the process of developing a social bond to prosocial others and prosocial activities has been interrupted by unconcerned or inconsistent parents, by poor school performance, or by inconsistent teachers, youths are more likely to come under the influence of peers who are in the same situation and are also more likely to be influenced by such peers to engage in delinquent activities. (p. 242)

The central variables of social developmental theory are opportunity for involvement (in the bonding process), skills (those necessary to perform competently in family, school, and prosocial peer settings), and reinforcements (rewards consequent to skill use in the involved settings). To the degree that such involvements, skills, and/or reinforcements are inadequate, the probability of delinquent behavior is purportedly enhanced.

Integrated Learning Theory

Feldman's (1977) comprehensive attempt to explore the sources of criminal and delinquent behavior is both multicomponent and multilevel in structure. Criminal behavior, he asserts, grows jointly from individual predisposition, social learning, and social labeling. Borrowing from Eysenck's (1977) views on inherited aspects of personality—especially temperament, conditionability, and the potential for conscience development—Feldman notes that both extroverted neurotics and persons high on psychoticism measures may have high crime potential. The former, Eysenck holds, have poor potential for adequate socialization; the latter may be insufficiently responsive to the distress of others. As Nietzel (1979) observes, "The potential criminal is someone whose genetically influenced personality predispositions make it difficult to acquire the classically conditioned avoidance responses which Eysenck held were the elemental components of human conscience and the ability to resist temptations to antisocial conduct" (p. 88).

Such individual predisposing factors set the stage, in effect, for the acquisition of delinquent behaviors. Learning processes further the acquisition—as well as the likelihood of both subsequent performance and maintenance—of the behaviors and include, in Feldman's view, both learning to offend and learning not to offend. Although diverse approaches to learning and behavior change are drawn upon in operationalizing the mechanisms at the heart of this perspective, social learning theory is its primary feature. Criminal behaviors (especially in genetically predisposed persons) are acquired, performed, and maintained largely as a function of the social learning processes identified in Table 1. Of additional consequence to the actual performance of criminal behaviors are such situational determinants as risk of detection, level of punishment if detection occurs, level of incentives, presence or absence of transgressive models, low self-esteem, nature of the victim, and alternative legitimate means to obtain gains:

> Thus, probability is greatest when detection is unlikely, punishment minimal, incentive high, alternatives are absent, transgressing models are present, the transgression requires little skill, the victim is both a stranger and unlikely to report the offense, and self-esteem is temporarily low. (Feldman, 1977, p. 103)

Once delinquent behavior is performed, its continuation is in part, according to Feldman, a function of social labeling. The labeling process and its purported consequences are conceptualized in integrated learning theory as described in our earlier consideration of social labeling theory.

Other Multicomponent Theories

Complementing the integrative efforts presented thus far, a number of additional investigators have sought to describe the etiology of juvenile delinquency in a manner more fully reflecting the apparent complexity of its roots. These efforts include Cohen and Land's (1987) criminal opportunity theory, which synthesizes control and differential opportunity theories; Kornhauser's (1978) social disorganization theory, which similarly blends control and strain propositions; Aultman and Wellford's (1978) combined model of control, strain, and labeling theories; Wilson and Hernnstein's (1985) incorporation of genetic predispositional and social learning influences; Elliott, Huizenga, and Ageton's (1985) "fully integrated model," consisting of control, strain, and social learning perspectives; Hogan and Jones's (1985) socioanalytic theory, seeking to blend structural sociological, social learning, psychoanalytic, symbolic interactionist, and biological conceptualizations; Warren's (1983) interpersonal maturity theory, combining strain, cultural deviance, control, and psychodynamic proposals; and the diversely composed, partial theory construction calls of Bahr (1979), Corning and Corning (1972), W. Glaser (1969), Himelhoch (1965), R. E. Johnson (1979), Rutter and Giller (1983), and West (1967). We strongly concur with this multicomponent perspective, for what we believe is its likely superior explanatory power as well as for its positive utilitarian implications for the design and implementation of effective delinquency interventions.

In the chapter that follows, we will present and illustrate the etiological perspectives of our sample of delinquent youths. Their own single-component and multicomponent theories will be offered and exemplified in detail, both for the phenomenological information they convey and in preparation for a later contrast and comparison with the academic perspectives on delinquency causation examined in this chapter.

CHAPTER 3

Causation:
Youth Perspectives

What do you think causes juvenile delinquency?

In the present chapter, the delinquent youths speak for themselves. Their answers reveal a quite broad and interesting array of perspectives—conventional and unconventional, expected and unexpected, naive and sophisticated. Diverse *family dysfunctions* were the most frequent factors cited, and we will present representative youth statements of this type first. The influence of *peers* (i.e., pressure, acceptance, and modeling) were also quite commonly suggested, as were etiologies associated with *drugs.* The latter concerned both drug-taking effects and money-seeking influences. Somewhat less common but not infrequent were causation notions focused upon *poverty, school,* or *labeling* considerations. A few youths responded more complexly and less monocausally, providing *multicomponent perspectives* typically involving family, peer, drug, and other proposed delinquency roots acting in combination. Finally, we will share quotations reflecting a substantial number of interesting and at times provocative youth-identified causes of delinquency, most of which were mentioned but once. Most of these offerings may be broadly categorized as either intrapersonal, familial, or environmental in focus. These several *miscellaneous* suggestions further concretize the sheer breadth of etiological perspectives offered by our participating youths.

The excerpts presented here are a sample of youth-offered "ordinary knowledge" selected from our study's 250 interviews on the basis of representativeness, clarity, and collective range of youth perspectives. Throughout the chapter, the interviewers' questions are indicated by italic type. The numbers at the end of each portion of interview material identify the various respondents.

FAMILY DYSFUNCTION

General Influence

What do you think makes kids get in trouble?

From the minute they're a baby and they grow up they see what their family does, and what their family does they're going to do.

OK, so you can do what your family does?

Yeah, that's their environment, that's how they grew up. If they grew up learning that stealing, doing drugs, drinking is good, then that's what they're going to do. If they grow up learning that going to school, graduating from school, going to college is good, that's what they're going to do 'cause that's their environment. (093)

I'd say about 75 percent of what all kids do is from what a parent teaches him. It is up to the parent to provide the training and education the kid needs to fight off the original potential to do bad. If the parental messages are missing, a kid doesn't really know what's right or wrong. About 25 percent of what a kid does is from his own personality or inner self. (016)

Harsh Parental Discipline

Parents, they think they be helping a kid by beating them, and it makes them worse.

How does it make them worse?

All the anger, he can't do nothing about being beat, so that anger just stays inside him.

Does it come out, does it make him more aggressive on the street?

Yes.

Why is that?

'Cause he feels pain, the pain gets too much for him. (051)

It could also be they could be brought up with physical neglect, where the parents is always beating up on them and they just made them go out and not care about them.

Why would that make that happen?

Because the kid is getting beat from being a toddler on. It could make the kid feel like beating and violence is what life is all about.

Like that is what is normal?

Yes, and he could think it is normal, and then when he goes to school or she goes to school and they might fight. And when the teacher or the principal gets that kid to the side and says, "Listen, you can't do that in my school," the kid might not understand. He might be like "Why can't I fight? My parents told me that it is right to fight," and he might not know any different. (091)

Do you feel a lot of [the problem] stems from the way your father punished you?

Yeah, for example, I was small and I saw—I was 6 or 7 years old—and I saw a can of red paint in the garage, and the guy across the street had just bought a brand new 1977 Trans Am. And I took the red paint and put a stripe down the side of the car. Now I could see getting a spanking for that, but not for the little things, like "Dad when's lunch? Dad, when's this?" I was young and I was interested and I kept asking questions, and sometimes he'd give me a smack and he'd just say, "Go sit down" or "Go and stop bothering me." I can see getting scolded for the paint on the car, but I can't see getting scolded for asking questions. (243)

So if somebody is nurtured and has love and care, they won't become a juvenile delinquent—is that what you're saying?

Yes, I would say that because you can say, for instance, like say your mother is alcoholic, she's always abusing you, you have no father, you have nobody there to look out for you, and the next thing you know you're out there robbing, your mother's in there on the couch—on the sofa—sleeping with a cigarette in her hand. Next thing you know you come in late, she wakes up, she beats you with the belt, you're in your room crying, have marks all over your body, and it encourages you to go out there and say, "I want to be put away. I don't want to be living with my mother because she abuses me. I want to be with somebody that cares about me." (137)

Lax Parental Discipline

What about the bad kids that you hung around with? Why do you think they were doing it?

I guess because most of the kids, their parents didn't care about them. They were always like outside, hanging around stealing stuff. I think that's because—I'm not saying their mother didn't love them, but nobody really had any control over them. Their parents didn't put their foot down. They didn't care, like they wouldn't care if they went out there and robbed somebody or beat somebody up, even when people would bring it to their attention. The parents would say, "Well, I can't do anything." I think that's one of the main reasons—because their parents don't care so they feel it's all right 'cause nobody tells them right from wrong. They just think it's fine like I did. Only it was different. My parents tried to put their foot down, but I didn't listen, so I think that's a big difference.

I think their mother should have put a curfew on things and put her foot down or even the father put his foot down 'cause like it's hard when a parent doesn't care 'cause when a parent doesn't care you can do what you want to do and nobody supervising you, nobody telling you right from wrong you just doing what you want. (021)

Was there anybody at home? Did anybody at your house notice that you had these things that you didn't have the money to buy? Was that a problem?

Yeah, my mom asked me where I got all the tapes, and I told her that my friends stole them for me. Sometimes they did, and sometimes I'd steal them for my friends. She knew I was shoplifting. She just could never catch me, and if she did catch me she really wouldn't have did that much, either. There's really nothing that she can do because she's my stepmom. My dad is usually the one that disciplines me, and I don't think he'd do anything. I mean they'd scold me and stuff, but they wouldn't ground me or anything unless I ripped off something big like a truck, and that's when I got grounded. (101)

Inconsistent Discipline

Well, let's just say you live with your mother, for instance, like I do, and you got into trouble. Your mother would tell you you're grounded for a month, and you know she never would go through with it. A half hour to an hour later or maybe even a day or two later, you know, you say, "Mom can I do this? Can I do that?" and she doesn't say you're grounded, she just says, "Yeah, go ahead." Say you rode your bike across the street when you were a kid and your mom says, "Well, you've lost it for a week." My mother would give it back the next day. All you would have to do is ask her about 100 times. With my father, you would not get it back for a week, and every time you ask and you were bugging him, you'd lose it for another week. (242)

Parental Rejection

Yes, but some parents can't talk to their children the way they should because, you know, they don't think it's gonna work or anything like that.

What could she have said differently?

Everything would be fine, that all my pain would go away, that I was gonna . . . hurt . . . but she never told me it would go away. She used to tell me she loved me. I know my mom loves me, but what hurts is that—one thing I'll never forgive her for was when I had got raped and I told her, I was scared to tell her at first, and when I did tell her I wanted her to believe me because it was true and she didn't.

She did eventually, didn't she?

Yes, she did, but I wanted her to believe me then. She should believe me over her boyfriend, and I don't think that it's right that she didn't because I'm her child and she should believe me. That's one thing I'll never forgive her for.

Did that make you angry? Your pain was one of the reasons, but then you were also angry?

Yes. And that's when I started doin' bad things, hanging around with the wrong crowd. Because I thought that my mom didn't love me or care about me. I know that she said she loved me, but I just didn't think she, you know, meant it. So I just started doin' things. (006)

One thing you said was abuse?

Yes, like not being around your parents or gettin' love that you see other kids get, and you start yourself saying, "Nobody cares about me." You could just do things to get attention, because it's the only way you could get it. (008)

Parental Oversolicitousness

That's true too, but it's not parents who don't care. Sometimes parents care too much, and they want to do and do for their kids. So at a certain point their kid starts getting spoiled and getting everything he wants, you know, and everything is going his way, you know, and sometimes the parents just can't say no to their kids. When a kid asks if he can go out and stay out until all hours of the night and the parents say yes, then they get in trouble in that period of time. It's the parenting; they have to know when to say no. Spoiling your kid or neglecting your kid, either one of those things can make a kid leave home and get into trouble. If you're spoiled and getting everything you want, that gives you a big opportunity to mess up and get into crime and be involved in negative things. And if you're neglected, that affects you emotionally, and you want to leave home because of your emotional state; that causes problems, too. (091)

Parental Disharmony

Is there anything that you think parents could do or your parents could have done—your stepdad and your mom—is there anything they could do now or could have done then to help you out of trouble?

Get a divorce when they got married. I got sick of hearing the arguing, constantly just at each other's throats, just yelling and screaming, and I didn't want to stay home. You know, that's why I was always out driving around, and that's when I picked up the tickets. A lot of them I should have fought and probably could have beat them. I just as soon would have paid for them and blown them off. No, I got sick of being home. I'd rather be out, away from home. I didn't like hearing my mom screaming. It gets tiring after a while, and my stepfather being the coward that he is, I just didn't like it. They could have argued sometime when I wasn't there. If they needed to argue, they could have left. I mean, it was my house, too. (105)

Family Violence

When I was 3 my mom left [my father] because he abused her. I saw him knock out her teeth, slam her against the wall, and he took me and my brother, rammed our heads together and sent us to our room. He wouldn't let me and my brother talk or anything. Like when my mother was sleeping, he'd come in and pull her hair if he wanted something. And my mother didn't do it, he'd hit her with a bottle or something. And I got a scar on my leg from his breaking a bottle. He's just abusive. And now, he's with a 13-year-old and that's not good. You can tell that something's wrong with him. (032)

OK, what do you think causes kids to become delinquent?

Sometimes it could be because problems at home, like fathers hitting on the children or hitting on the mother. Or it could be that the parents don't pay much attention to them. Or it could be a boyfriend who could be hitting on you also. It could be a lot of things. (050)

Single Parenting

See, it depends on how the kid is raised, single parent, or how the parent treats them, like when they were younger, and that has a lot to do with how the parents raise them—you know, how their life is with the parents.

All right, so you mentioned the family there or the environment. If a kid has a single parent like you mentioned, what difference does that make?

It makes a big difference. The mother gets tired and a lot of problems go on. The mother, slowly but sure, she gets tired of the same problems and she slacks up on the kid, and the more slack she gives him, he'll take advantage of it 'cause he's young. He wants to experience everything in life, so he experiments with things. (045)

Before, when you started, you said it had something to do with family. Can you elaborate on that?

Like, if your father leaves your home you usually take it upon yourself just to go out and do whatever you want, 'cause you figure your mother, she ain't gonna do nothing about it. But if your father still lives home, he lays down the rules and tells you what you can do and what you can't do, and you usually listen to your father. Sometimes your family's broken up, and you think, "What the hell, I might as well go out and do it anyways. I've got nothing, my family's already broken up and they've proved me wrong, so I might as well prove them wrong." (053)

Family Disconnectedness

No, I would just want to sit home. You know, with the family, that's it. Like dinnertime, my father eats in the living room, my mother eats at the table with me and my sister, and my father's in the other room watching wrestling or boxing on TV. You know, it's obvious that it's not going to be a perfect family.

Where do you get your idea of a perfect family?

Like my aunt and uncle, they're perfect. They have like no problems. You know, they're just like—they have three boys, they sit at the table, they go out to baseball or whatever. We never do nothin' like that. My father is always saying, "Oh, I'm too busy, this and that." When I was living with my grandmother, we went on vacations every summer. And my sisters just stayed home with my mother and father and don't do anythin' . You know, it's no excitement. It's not like a family, it's just people living in one house. I walk in the door and they don't even say "Hi." Don't even say "Good morning." It's not even close. So the perfect family for me would be like getting up, saying hello, good morning, talking when you need somebody to talk to. Or just being there, you know.

I was gonna sit there and say that's a television family, but you've actually seen what a family is like.

My father's sister is just like that, they go on vacations every summer, they eat at a table, they don't even fight. I never saw them fight, never, ever in my life. (044)

Well, you could send your kids to an after school program, and they could do things until their parents come home from work. Then your parent might have time to talk to their child and ask them, "How was your day?" and things like that.

If you could just have talked to them, would you have been a delinquent?

Me, no.

No, you wouldn't have or no, that's not right?

No, if I could have talked to them, I wouldn't have been a delinquent.

That's all it would have taken to keep you from becoming delinquent?

Sort of, yes, and following instructions, that would have kept me from being a delinquent. (048)

Parental Models

When you were doing things, did you think you were being delinquent or were you aware of the bad things?

I wasn't aware of it at the time. I would say to myself, "Well, I'm doing this because I want to be older and it's not anything bad." I see my uncle do it, I see my mommy do it. So therefore I do it. I want to be grown up, too, like them. But then as soon as I got older I understood that the things that I did do were delinquent and wrong and sometimes even harmful to others and myself. (014)

OK, what do you think causes delinquency?

I think what causes delinquency is when you—the kids fall into temptations and when they brought up in a kind of environment and they try to see what their parents do and they role model after their parents and do what their parents does. (017)

Sibling Models

I say another part, too, is not only the parents, but the older brother, older sister. You know, the young ones always admire the oldest, that's got to be a big part, too. Older brother giving the role model to the younger one, the younger one most of the time always like to follow the big brother in his steps, and if the big brother is doing negative stuff or the big sister, eventually the young one will get into the same trouble or the same gang.

All right, so, in addition to the parent, the older brothers and sisters can have an impact, too. If they are acting negative, acting delinquent, chances are a younger brother or sister may also act that way. Why do you think the younger brothers or sisters would do that? I mean, is it important for them to be like their older brothers or sisters?

Maybe 'cause the parent gives like the ones who are acting negative maybe more slack. You know she's strict on the young one, and the young one figures if maybe he acts like the older one, he thinks maybe he'll get the same slack, you know, no curfews. (045)

Why do they [engage in delinquent behavior]?

Do it to have money in they pockets or just to be doing it. Think it's fun.

Why are kids like that?

'Cause they been little, like they probably have older sisters or older brothers that been out there doing the same thing as they. As they grew up their big brother or sister was doing the same thing, so when they grew up they wanted to be the same way. Like the oldest, so I guess that's how it is. (025)

PEERS

Peer Pressure

A kid wants to be accepted, so he will do what the other kids are doing even if he knows it's wrong. He doesn't want to be embarrassed or disrespected by refusing to do something. On the other hand, he doesn't want to be seen doing something good or positive, then he'll get ridiculed for it. The people I knew and hung out with would really disrespect you and sometimes hurt you if you didn't do what they wanted you to. There's a code among friends, and if you want to be with them, then you do *everything* they say and you cover up and look out for each other. This means lying and doing a lot of illegal stuff. If you don't they will hurt you and disrespect you, ridicule you and use you in any way they can. It's unbelievable pressure. You have to work your way up within a gang. You do this by doing everything they want. This means dressing like them, acting like them, and looking like them. (040)

Yes, and there is also peer pressure. If I got a friend, they say, "If you're not going to be my friend, then get away from me," and they'll do anything to get this person to be a friend. And what's happening is that the person will cause you or you will cause the other person to do something. Like if you're supposed to go into a store and you say, "Let's rob the store," you know it's bad, they say, "You're not my friend, get away from me—I don't want to see you again." And you get stuck in your head, "Well, gee, this is my friend and I got to help him out." What happened was he pulled you into getting in trouble because he might give you a gun and say, "Well, hold up this person," and you might get

caught because the cops are waiting outside for you and from
there you get in trouble because you got caught with the gun. . .
(002)

So you are also saying peers had something to do with it?

It was peer pressure, a lot of peer pressure. That's one of the
hardest ones, I fell right into it.

You wanted to belong?

Yes, I wanted to belong.

*You wanted to be down, in other words—to be in with the in crowd
and to be like they are?*

Yeah.

So what happened as a result?

Well, the in crowd started getting more rowdy and stuff like that.
Like the more rowdy you get, it seemed like the more people
would join, like me. Everybody wanted to be down, so once
everybody started being down, slowly but surely things started
falling out of place. People were getting shot at, some people got
locked up, and after the first person got locked up, some people
quit. But some people keep on going until some more people get
locked up and everything was falling off.

Did you want to get locked up?

No, I thought I never would get locked up, I thought I never
would.

Was there ever a point that you were frightened?

Yes, many times. There was a couple of shootings going around,
people shooting up on the block.

*But even though you were afraid and all these things were happening,
you never at any time wanted to get out, to stop?*

No, 'cause I wasn't talking to anybody, that's what I wanted to
do. I wanted to stay with the in crowd.

At any cost?

Yes, back then I would go to any cost to stay with the in crowd,
any cost. (111)

The friends that I've had you really can't call them friends, you can call them like my drinking buddies, my drug dealer friends and stuff, and a lot of them are in jail now, including my ex-boyfriend.

Why did you hang around with them?

I don't know. I was never really accepted because I wasn't up to style and my parents were poor and everything. And I wasn't accepted into the preppie society, and I wasn't accepted in jock because I didn't act like them. I wasn't a cheerleader or gorgeous. You know, I had my own traits and people couldn't understand that I was an individual because where I went to school everybody cliqued. If you didn't belong to a clique you weren't anybody. If you didn't dress like somebody else or look like somebody else or something you weren't anything, so the friends I got were the friends that didn't belong to anything. So where I was accepted was with the burnout kids, because I was a burnout, plain and simple. I was a punk and everything, and I used to dress wicked wild. I still wear my basic black because that's my favorite color, but a lot of things I did weren't accepted by a lot of the people, and in the burnout you could kill your mother and father and they wouldn't care.

They would accept you for whoever you were. Did they pressure you—like was there pressure from the burnout group to be a burnout?

Yeah, if you didn't do drugs you weren't in it, if you didn't drink you weren't in it, if you didn't do a lot of stuff you weren't in it, and then you were a nerd. I'd rather be a burnout than a nerd. (093)

Peer Acceptance

Even me myself. A lot of my peers made me feel that I was wanted more than I felt at home. The littlest thing could happen at home that made me feel that my friends liked me better than my own family. And I would just turn to them. And you turn to them more and more. You become bad. (036)

Did you find that peers were more important than family?

Most likely, yeah.

Why? I mean, what was so important about them?

'Cause with them I could get respect, or you get respect from them or the people on the street.

You keep going back to getting respect. What kind of respect were you looking for?

Respect so you know, like instead of anybody down the street and bothering you they know who you be with and so if they don't want no trouble with you because of the people you hang with.

OK, so it's also like you've got protection?

Yeah, protection. (083)

I think it's the environment because most of the time they don't want to stay home. They want to be with their friends and all their friends want them to do stuff and they do it mainly for their friends. They want to be down and they want to act cool. They want to be down with this gang and not with the other guys. (043)

Why did you hang around with the wrong people?

To act like I was cool and everything, because I wasn't satisfied at home and I just felt my parents didn't love me. I would go out and find my love this way. (032)

Peer Modeling

Putting together from people you have seen and people you have known, what would you say are the major causes that you have seen of juvenile delinquency?

Peer pressure and the environment because my friends, personally, they are not used to adapting to other environments. Adapting to maybe goodness. They are so far down in the ghettos that it is almost like they can't reach out for help anymore. They can get the help if they still try, but a lot of them are now inside prisons, inside lockups because of the fact they committed serious crimes. And it was all due to the environment they were brought up in. They were always brought up around people that were into trouble, and then they followed that pattern. And they are now more or less the ones out there getting into trouble, showing the younger generation how to get into trouble. And it is kind of like a chain reaction. It goes down to each generation. (151)

What do you think causes kids to become delinquent?

I think what caused them to become delinquent is when they see their friends doing things like that or maybe adults who do drugs or something, they want to find what it's like to do that. And then when it gets around to their other friends, they all think they're cool or something, and they do that to try to be in the crowd and be older and look older and things. I think that's how—what causes other people to do it. (031)

You said the environment and people they see.

Right. The people—like if everybody around them is doing one sort of thing, then they gonna want to do that, too. I think it's basically the role models, role model problems, not having good people around like how you all are here. That's what my problem was. (073)

Some neighborhoods kids live in are wild. Stealing is normal and a way of life. If you need food or clothing, you just steal. When little kids are growing up, they see this going on all the time and think it's normal and that's the way it should be. (018)

OK, what do you think causes juvenile delinquency?

I think it's mainly the environment around you. The people that you're with, the people that live around you. For instance, if you go outside and everyone around you is delinquent, the only value you have is to be delinquent because that's how everybody is. (036)

DRUGS

Drug-Taking Effects

So how do the kids go from being and having troubles in the home and then being out? Why do they slide to the drugs?

Well, first of all, the people that they hang out with, they'll run away and they'll find someone to stay with. They see that person taking drugs and things, and they start getting curious and wondering, "I wonder how I'll feel if I try it?" Or they'll say, "Well, I scared to take it" and things, and then they'll pressure them like "Go ahead, take it. Nothin' will happen, I'm here, you know I won't let nothin' happen to you. If somethin' happens I know what to do, I'll give you milk or somethin' like that." And after a while, maybe sometimes they'll take a couple of drugs just to see how you feel and not to overdo it and then, you know, after a while, since it's been OK and nothin' happened, they'll constantly take it and then, you know, they start feeling an attraction towards it and they'll get addicted to it. I guess that's one of the reasons they'll get addicted to it.

From the addiction to drugs other things occur?

Right, robbery and murder and things like that when they really needed it bad. Especially crack. I used to take it myself, and it gets in your system in 8 seconds and lasts about a minute or two. And it feels—and after a while you take it, you get depression and want more, and then it makes you feel dirty and not wanted and things like that. It makes you feel YUCK! (004)

OK, good. Let's get started now. Just relax and let's enjoy this. OK, what is your opinion on why kids get into trouble?

Well, why most kids get in trouble is the uses of drugs and alcohol. It's so popular with teenagers now, and a lot of kids are getting involved with it, and while they are under the influences they are doing a lot of stuff they normally wouldn't do.

Because they get hyped up, does it make them braver?

They're not in their right minds. (060)

The reason why I say it hits you hard, which I wanted to say this—once you get high on it you feel good, and the high only stays for no less than 3 minutes and no more than 6 minutes, and it's a high that you never want to come down again so people say it's better than having sex. You get really depressed when you come down, and that's why you'll rob your family or your loved ones, and after you spent the money and do what you do, you feel like, suicide runs through your mind, a lot of different things run through your mind—selling things, doing crimes to get away from the community you're in.

OK, so you see drugs as having a big part in delinquency.

Yes.

So, obviously, if drugs weren't available or around, there may not be as many kids getting into trouble. Do you believe that?

Yes I do. I say 90 percent of the kids in New York City,

correction DFY [Division for Youth] kids, half of them wouldn't be here if they didn't take drugs. It's a lot of money. It's like a business. It's like an elevator—you go up and you come down. You can never stay up there when you're on drugs. (045)

Yeah, because when you're taking drugs you do a lot of things you wouldn't do when you're straight. Like I did a couple crimes that I probably wouldn't have even dreamed of doing if I wasn't on acid. Sometimes beer can do it to you. I think that's a lot of kids' problems, too. They get influenced by drugs and they just start getting in trouble, 'cause when I was on acid I was doing everythin'. . . (097)

I used to sit there popping pills, smoking up, drinking, all at the same time. I remember one time I was so fucked up I almost killed my grandmother. I almost threw her out the second-floor window because I was gone, I didn't even know what the hell I was doing.

Is that a feeling that people like to achieve?

No, see, when I used to get high, it used to make me forget everything in the world that I hated, and it used to make me feel good. Then when I started doing so much, it didn't make me feel good anymore, it just made me feel like I wanted to kill myself.

So it started out taking you away from yourself, then later it made it really bad. Were you getting in trouble when you were using the drugs?

Well, I didn't really start stealing and skipping school until I started taking the drugs in November of 1985. Three weeks after we started doing drugs I got arrested for the first time.

If drugs get you in trouble, why do you use drugs to begin with?

Because it was cool. I remember in eighth grade talking in school on a Friday about how we were going to get fried that night. Didn't care if the teachers were listening. One time when they tried to take me back to school, the principal shoved me in the classroom and I punched him in the stomach, and then he dragged me in the classroom and I kicked him, and then I just kicked him again and I ran out of the school and I never went back to school. (093)

Money-Seeking Effects

You grew up a lot in New York City. What did you see on the streets that could maybe get other kids in trouble?

Dope dealers in cars. They see 'em riding in Mercedes, BMWs, every day coming in with different kinds of gold, dope fiends coming over to them giving them all kinds of VCRs, of gold, TVs for just a lousy bag of heroin. And they see that and they get influenced. That's what they see. That's the influence, the guy that's selling the drugs.

So you think it would help to stop a lot of trouble on the street if they did something about the drug dealers?

Yes, not only the dope dealers but the parents. The parents could be on dope. They see their parents go into a certain place every day, they gonna wonder who runs that certain place. They gonna say, "One of these days when I grow up I'm gonna go over there and see what's going on in there." They probably see their parents taking the drugs or whatever, and they just get influenced by their parents. And in NYC the parents are paying attention to drugs and what's going on around the block and they just forget about their kids, they just leave 'em. They hungry—"Mama, I want some food"—they say, "I'll get to you later, later," and when the time comes they just forget about their kids, and if they can't make their money for the drugs, how are they gonna feed the kids? (058)

Drugs played a lot of things on my part because I was always hard up for drugs and I had no ways of obtaining money, so I either stole it to get money or just ripped people off or just hang around with people with money or beat up people with money. That's why most people do crimes. (149)

Drugs and alcohol—do they have any effect on kids' getting into trouble?

I say yeah, 'cause like I said before there's a lot of drugs out there, and kids look at that as being the faster way to make money in a fancy way by walking around the block with a whole bunch of money in your pocket, a beeper hanging off your pocket, stuff like that. You know, some people see themselves getting more respect by selling drugs and stuff, by selling it to people, stuff like that. Being as long as they make their money it doesn't really make a difference to them, as long as money keep coming in and they get paid for what they out there doing, even though they out there taking a chance on their life, or going to jail and never seeing the streets again.

OK, you're talking about the selling end of it. How about the using end of it? Do kids who use drugs and alcohol—does that have an effect on the trouble they get into?

Yes it do, 'cause you know some people, they get a habit, they start fiending.

What do you mean by fiending?

They get you to addict, you know they need it, they can't do without drugs. If they don't have drugs they'll go out there and start robbing and stuff like that. If they don't got no money or nothing like that to get their drugs, that's where certain kids will go out there robbing stuff and girls go out there standing on corners and stuff like that or doing crazy stuff just to get money to get their drugs. (057)

I used to deal, for a while, the smaller stuff. I didn't deal crack, just easy stuff. It's so easy to sell it 'cause you buy it and you sell it not even meaning to, to one of your friends, and they just keep coming back to you, and each time you buy it you've got more money so you just keep going higher and higher and buying more and more from your person, so the person you buy it from becomes a dealer, too. So it just kind of makes a chain right down the line unless you buy it from a dealer already. You make so much money it's hard to stop because you just want to make more money. (091)

POVERTY

Why do you think kids get into trouble?

I think kids get in trouble because, while they are growing up, their parents have low-income jobs and housing, and they see that they are not getting enough. And they see other people making money, and they have nowhere to turn to, so they think the only way to get the things that they want to get is by robbing and stealing. And they think if they steal it will make them feel higher. So that is what they rob for. (133)

Why would they rather steal?

'Cause they probably can't get the things they want from their families, so they probably said, "So if I can't have that, I'll go out and rob a rich person and go rob stores." And they probably tell all their friends when they come back with a lot of jewelry that they bought this and I bought that, but they really didn't. (019)

OK, as I mentioned to you earlier here, we are doing an interview, and basically we just want to get in your own words why kids get into trouble. Can you tell me some of your reasons or thoughts around that?

First of all, money.

Money?

Yes, that's the main thing, everybody wants to get some money. And they see a quick way of gettin' it, so they just go for it and get in trouble.

So there's a need out there to have money, and in order to fill that need, kids end up stealing.

Sellin' drugs, stealin' from their family, all kinds of stuff . . .

A lot of people—just about everybody has a need for money. Why do kids end up involved in crime to get it? There's other ways to get money without being involved in crime.

'Cause nobody comes around and say, "Here, do you want a job and you want to work such and such?" Plus we young, 15, you can't fill out no application for no job, none of that. So I think that this is the best thing that's happened to me, to get locked up here. Now when I leave I gonna applicate and they gonna hook me up with a job or whatever, and now I'm 16, now it's gonna be easy. Before, 15, 14 and not be with money, sell some drugs and do whatever to get some money. You know, a dude give you like 100 dollars every 3 weeks or whatever and you could get it, you know. So it's an easy way of gettin' it, so you just do it. (066)

We are seeking your views regarding the causes of juvenile delinquency and also ways to prevent it or at least reduce it. The first question I would like to ask you is why do you think youths get in trouble?

Because sometimes youth don't have money, they want money to wear nice clothes to school. That's one of the main reasons why I got in trouble, because I wanted nice things and my family couldn't afford it for me, so I got into drugs because it was a way to get money, and I needed money. (115)

I believe that children get in trouble because they start thinking they be getting things for free. Most of them start at a young age. They start hanging around with a bad group, the ones that start taking candy out of the store. You know, they start taking candy out the store and they think they can get it free. So most of them start doing that more and more often, even with their mother. Then they start taking things more bigger, like bikes, anything they see. Even when they go in their friends' house, they are taking. So when they grow up, that is one of their favorite things. So when they get teenage, they are breaking into houses, taking cars. They want to take everything they can take. I believe they start stealing because they think if they steal, they can save money. They get stuff in return without paying a dime for it. (128)

Some people steal because—maybe because they don't have a job. Maybe they greedy and just want to go out there and steal. Some people steal because they lack money and they don't have a family that they can connect to get that money from. (023)

SCHOOL

So, in other words, you don't think the system is working, kids are not learning . . . How does this affect him doing crimes?

If he ain't learning, he gonna do crime.

Why? What do you feel is that connection?

Because the kid is gonna get stupider and stupider. They gonna go out there and do something stupid. He ain't gonna know how to read, he gonna read the sign backward and get hit by a car while he cross the street. He gonna get a crack paper that says don't use crack, he'll think it says use crack. If it says don't sell drugs, he'll probably do it. (113)

Do schools help prevent delinquency, or do they help cause it?

Well, um, sometimes they help cause it. Like if a kid has a problem and some teachers say go to them and they'll help them out. But they don't do that. They either scared or they just very aggressive, and they think they gonna hurt them. Like sometimes kids are scared to go to them because they think they're gonna tell on them or not give them good advice and think they don't understand. Sometimes they don't and sometimes they do. And you know, some kids would think that they're not gonna understand. Sometimes the teacher treats them like "Well, let me pass them so they don't have to be in my class," or they'll say, "Your hands hurt, you don't have to write, just sit there for a couple of minutes" or somethin' like that. And they'll just keep on. They'll just give you somethin' to keep you out of their way, and things like that. (004)

LABELING

So what you were trying to say is that you think adults should not judge young people as much as they do?

Yeah, I think they should get to know somebody before they judge them. You know, you can look at a book cover, and if it doesn't look good, you can put that book aside. But if you start reading it or read the back of it, you might learn that this might be a good book. I think they jump the gun too soon because there's a lot of good people out there and a lot of us are teenage. They can be helped, and, you know, a lot of the time somebody has looked at somebody and said he's a bad person. You know, after a while, after a couple of years of hearing you're a bad person, I feel, you know, you're gonna be a bad person because that's just how society accepts you.

So what the adults are saying about you, you think will influence how you are?

Yeah, unless you are really stubborn and say, "Hey, I'm not like that." But when you got the whole society calling you bad, I mean, what else can you do? You know everything you do and everything you try to do, they're still gonna be calling you bad, you know. Say a kid has been in trouble all his life and he goes out and rescues someone, you know, saves his life. He ain't gonna get as much credit as someone goody-two-shoes go out and save someone's life. Same situation, just two different people. He's gonna get more recognition because he's been a good child all his life, but the kid on the other hand that's been in trouble, he ain't gonna get as much recognition, and I don't think that's fair. A good example may be somebody that's raped someone. Maybe there was something wrong and he got fixed, but in society, he gonna go and people shy from him because he is a raper. You know, maybe he's fine now, but he's really never gonna have that chance. You know, he's never really gonna be able to prove himself because everybody's gonna be going, "Bad person, bad person," keep away from him. I don't think that's fair. I think society hangs on to crimes people do. People make mistakes. (105)

My father he was in [a state delinquency facility] when he was a kid, then he went into the marines. I don't know how he got an honorable discharge because they kicked him out. He threw somebody over a balcony or something like that. When he got home he went to prison for conspiracy to extort, and then he got out and he passed away. So I grew up in pretty much the same neighborhood where he got shot, and I grew up with a lot of people telling me that my father was a bad man, and it kind of reflected on me because a lot of people knew who he was. They tried to influence me to be like him; they wanted me to be more like him. They thought it was cool that he was in prison or that he was a part of the Mafia or whatever. (099)

Peer pressure, when you go to school and meet different people and see different things, and you meet more friends and you try to fit in the best way you can, and if you don't fit in with the first group you try the next group, and the next group might be negative and the only way for you to fit in is to do what they're doing, like causing trouble.

What did you have to do to fit into the good group?

You had to go to school, don't cause fights, do your homework, be quiet. You have to be quiet to fit into the quiet group.

So you have the good group up here and the bad group down there and you try out, and if you don't fit, you try out for the other one?

Yeah.

Why didn't you fit into the good group?

Because all my life I was doing bad things, and all the kids knew I was a troublemaker. They thought, "She's just coming to start trouble," so even when I tried to change I couldn't because there wasn't anyone to believe you. (030)

You can't put a label on a kid forever. Once you put that label on, they know the guy's reputation, so you carry it out. They feel they have expectations to carry out to keep that label. Like if you call somebody a thief, and they try to tell you they are not a thief, to show you they are not a thief. But you constantly call them a thief, so they resort to the things that a thief would do. They steal. (154)

How do you think kids who are currently involved in juvenile delinquency in the community see themselves or think about their life-style?

Most of them think like they're nothing.

What do you mean by nothing?

Well, kind of like they're shit to everybody because that's what everybody tells them. You know, you're a no-good nothing. Most parents who don't understand their kids or how their kids are getting into this, or don't understand why it's their kids . . . you know, "You're terrible," "You're good for nothing," and then they go around thinking that about themselves. (233)

MULTICOMPONENT PERSPECTIVES

Peers, Drugs, Parents, Inhibition

OK, Barbara, do you have any idea what causes delinquency?

It could be peer pressure, and kids that's on drugs, problems with parents at home and not being able to express your feelings. (028)

Peers, Drugs, Parents, Absence of Support

Think about the other kids you know that are in trouble. What do you think caused them to get in trouble?

Taking drugs, and hanging around with the wrong people, family situations and no one helping them out. (032)

Peers, Drugs, Parents, School

OK, Helen, what's your opinion of why kids get in trouble?

I think mainly it's because of peer pressure. A lot of teenagers get tempted into negative things that they see their peers doing in the community—drugs, alcohol, cigarette smoking, shoplifting. Therefore, if they think their peers can do it, they think they can do it also. And many times their parents may not stop them, and they say, "If my parents are not going to stop me, then that makes it OK for me to do." Therefore they do it. I think that if they were disciplined more in the home that they wouldn't do it as much. But there are some kids at home that are disciplined, but I think that it's their choice, they make that choice to become delinquent. And I think that when they go to school and things, um, they might be influenced by the negative things they see at school. Maybe skipping school and things like that. So when they skip school with their other peers, that makes them maybe want to take drugs if their friends take drugs and things like that. (014)

Peers, Drugs, Parents, School, Abuse

What do you think causes kids to be delinquent?

Maybe they haven't been taught anything better than those values that they have to do those bad things. I think most of it is caused by—some of them feel, they don't feel cared for, and they have a lot of family problems, and they don't know how to deal with them. Or they don't have a good education, they don't like to go to school. I think that's what most of the problem of delinquency is. I think that maybe kids get hung up with the wrong people and the wrong crowd, and that causes delinquency a lot 'cause they want to fit in with their peer groups. Drugs caused it for a lot of people that I knew . . . drugs caused them to do more things. And when they started going out to parties and hanging out with the crowd causes a lot of delinquency 'cause they like to do a lot of bad things.

Something else that causes delinquency?

Being abused. I think that causes delinquency. People that's abused don't feel too good about themselves, especially young teenagers. They don't care too much about themselves, and they don't care what they do. Sometimes it can lead them to drinking or staying out, or not coming home at all, or disrespecting their parents. I think that causes a lot of delinquency. (038)

Peers, Drugs, Parents, School, Poverty, Neighborhood Norms

Definitely peer pressure—you may have a friend and he has a friend who is into stealing. They talk about it when you're there.

You don't want to seem soft, so you agree to do something with them. If you don't, they will disrespect you and tell everyone about it. It's important for kids to feel respected by their friends and to have a lot of status. If they have to, they will compete to see who can do a bigger crime. This makes them feel good, especially in front of girls. Once you pull it off, you think it was easy and you're not as scared the next time.

Another reason is not having money. Kids, even young ones 10 or 11 years old, want money. They like to show it off, and they want to have it so they can be independent and do what they want. They don't want to rely on their parents to give it to them. In most cases they know their parents don't have it to give to them. If they have money, it's a sign of power and status. They buy things and look important.

Some kids get hooked up with drugs or alcohol mainly from peer pressure and for the thrill of the moment. They don't think about tomorrow. When they're drunk or high they don't think, and they act stupid. A lot of kids don't know how dangerous drugs are; they see other kids doing it, so they feel it's cool and OK. All of these reasons are more important and considered first before a kid thinks about the risk involved. Once they are hooked on drugs, they need more money, and that leads to even more problems.

Some neighborhoods kids live in are wild. Stealing is normal and is a way of life. If you need food or clothing, you just steal. When little kids are growing up, they see this going on all the time and think it's normal and that's the way it should be. If they moved out of that neighborhood to a calmer, more normal area, they would start off stealing and acting wild, but I believe they would slowly learn not to steal.

School is another problem. They have these hooky parties where everyone skips. If you don't go they make fun of you and tell you about all of the fun you missed. So next time you go. Some kids don't go at all. They sit at home and do nothing all day or hang out with other kids who are not doing anything positive. Sooner or later they're going to get into trouble. Once they start skipping, it's harder to go back and you just say, "The hell with it." They get bored and are looking for something to do.

The type of family and parents a kid has is important also. A lot of homes only have one parent, usually the mother. The mother says things to the older kids like "Why don't you get a job?" or "I could use some help around here." So the older kid will go out and steal some groceries to help out the family. In other families kids are abused or neglected, so they grow up being angry or hateful. Instead of taking it out on their parents, they take it out on others and will rob or steal. They may also run away from home, and then they have to steal or do something illegal just to survive. (073)

MISCELLANEOUS

Intrapersonal

Bad Genes

Human nature, you know, you get some of the bad genes in some of the people and you get some of the good people. In order to be good you've got to be better than somebody. You know, if somebody's out there killing people he's bad and if somebody's working then they're good, so I don't think there will ever be no end to juvenile delinquency. (089)

My father, he was in facilities when he was a kid and he was in prison, and a lot of people say my father was passed down to me. (099)

Sometimes it runs in the family—like if the father was somebody who liked to beat up people and all that, sometimes it runs in the family and the kids get it, and they'll start doing it, too. (221)

Fun

What do you think causes kids or juveniles out there in the street—why do you think they get in trouble?

Because it's fun—it's fun while you do it.

It's enjoyable to do those kinds of things?

Yeah, 'cause when you look at it, driving a car fast or getting drunk, that type of stuff be fun to people, so we just do it. (089)

. . . when they do run away they'll need food or something and they'll steal it maybe, and when they do have a free chance of going somewhere you know they want to do something, you know, fun, exciting. Stealing is kind of fun, kind of except when you get in trouble for it. I like stealing, you know. I always shook when I did it but 'cause you're always afraid when you did that you're gonna get caught when you do steal it, so you shake and stuff. (103)

But you had the gymnastics and piano.

It did help me, but when I didn't go, that's when I became delinquent.

Why did you stop going?

Why did I stop? Because I see that they were doing bad stuff and I wanted to see how it was, so I would go and just have fun. (012)

So the bad stuff and the bad things looked like more fun to you.

Thrill

For the thrill of it all. A lot of kids, myself included, look at it as a thrill. An abusive family will make a kid run away a lot, and once on the street a kid has to live. After a while he finds the streets more exciting and attracting than putting up with all the bullshit at home. (064)

Boredom

Why do you think youths get in trouble?

Because they don't be busy—like to stay out of trouble they could go to like a day-care center, keep things moving. But since they want to hang out on the street, they see other people doing bad stuff and they say, "Oh, they making money," so they say they want to do it.

So it's being around and doing nothing and then seeing other kids making money?

Yep. (113)

Power

Yeah, the people you're around. I guess you get power from being that way. I'm assuming.

Power from being delinquent?

Yeah, you feel like you belong to something 'cause it's like the majority is delinquent and that's the way you want to be, too. (034)

Notoriety

Everyone in the neighborhood knows the badasses. That gives you a name, notoriety—good or bad. No one knows average Joe. (065)

Oppositional Feelings

Other things are people harping on you. Like you see on television, just say no to drugs. Everybody has some rebellion to drugs. You keep seeing slogans. Just say no to drugs. Just say no to drugs. Why? Is it that bad that they want to put all these things up to just say no to drugs? Maybe I should try it to see why they are telling me to say no. That is the same thing with teen pregnancy. A lot of it is, you see all the negativity with teen pregnancy. I bet you there is more teen pregnancy now than there was way back before when people weren't talking about it a lot. I think that has to do with it a lot. (146)

OK, it is like saying, "Don't look under that box." You are going to look under the box.

Familial

Providing Financial Help

They try to help their moms out, you know. Their moms ain't got nothing, but they want to help their moms and they don't know how to help. They get out there and they rob and they steal and stuff like that, and they end up getting locked up, or they either get killed for snatching jewelry, stuff like that. (057)

Intergenerational Transmission

Right! And it depends on the community and how you been trained from your family. My friends, older people, tell me that maybe your parents raised you like that because they were raised like that. Like my mother always says she used to be a black sheep of the family. And I understand how she feels 'cause my grandmother, she very strict and she still treat her out of the ordinary. And that's why sometimes she's like that, I understand that. It's just that you know she has to understand now it's time to change 'cause she old enough to understand what's right from wrong or at least try to stop what she's doin', you know. Some mothers, they don't care, or it's too hard for them to stop what they doing, and they don't know how to stop when no one doesn't give them no help, and the friends that they have help them continue the wrong things that they do. (004)

Racism

Like being brought up into a racial family or something like that. You'll go out and make racial acts. Like if I see a White man walking down the block, my first impression or my first thought is to either rush him, beat him up, or rob him. Make him somehow feel the hurt. (239)

Expressive Act

Those are delinquent behaviors. Why do kids fight and get in trouble?

Because they can't express their feelings toward their parents, so instead they go out and fight and steal and, you know, have sexual intercourse and do things to express their feelings instead of coming and telling their parents how they feel—telling their parents, "I disagree with this and that," but they go out and do something. (048)

Teen Fatherhood

You know, another thing that would probably get a kid into trouble is early pregnancy. Girls are having babies at a young age. You know, that probably has a big effect on the young man who is supposed to be the father. He'd have a problem of having no education and he be trying every way he can to survive to support his self and his child like every man should. So that would probably have a big effect on him. (045)

Failure to Be Physically Punished

But then again, you get the kids that think, "Well, my parents never hit me, so they must not care about me." Because they see on television shows where "Well, I hit you because I love you, and I want you to be set straight." Their parents think, "I never hit my kid." They never get hit and feel like they are missing something. Their parents don't care. They would at least hit them once in a while. They keep trying to do things wrong to see if their parents are going to hit them, to see if they cared, and they find they don't care and then they don't need them anymore. I have my friends. (148)

Environmental

Seeking Respect

Poor kids have nothing to lose, so they do crazy things to purposely get looked up to. Rich kids got too much to lose. (135)

Older Youth Influence

Older peer groups are attractive to younger kids. You feel like a big guy. They treat you that way, like you are important. Then they in return expect you to do crimes for the benefit of them. That's what happened to me. They used me to do a lot of jobs because the younger kid is less often caught, and once caught, is let off real easy. (011)

Police Abuse

When you walk in a store the policemen watch you like a hawk, and that makes a younger person want to steal. It's just how much they can get away with, being at the age that they are, and everything makes them want to challenge them. I know myself, I see a cop and he gonna say a certain thing to me, and I'm gonna look at him and say, "Fuck you," like excuse my language, but that's what I say. You know, he looking and you gotta make your comments. I can beat the shit out of you, why don't you be a man and do this and that. I don't have to, you know, they get paid and my father works and, you know, my mother works same as everybody else. It's the taxpayers' money they get paid with, and it should be all for one, not two for two, if you know what I'm saying by that.

Yeah, so you'd like the police maybe not to be on kids' backs all the time.

Yeah. (037)

Movies

OK, anything else? You mentioned environment. Were you referring to parents and peers as the environment, or are there other things in the environment that can cause delinquency?

I even think places that people go to and movies and things are very influential on what students do and what children do. Because I think movies kind of glorify a lot of delinquent behaviors and values and it makes it look really good and like appeals to the children, and they want to do it and they do, and then they break the law and things. (009)

Television

What actually in the streets would influence how somebody behaves? In other words, what would cause a youngster to commit a crime in the streets?

They probably like saw it on a TV show. Like with guns shooting people on a TV show and if they got a gun, they gonna shoot somebody out in the street or like a bank robber, they see a bank robber and they gonna rob a bank.

So kids see crimes committed on TV, and that's one reason why they might do it?

Yep. (117)

Why do you think they get attracted to the negative groups rather than the positive groups?

Well, I think a lot of it has to do with TV. Like when I watch TV, like "Miami Vice" or something like that, it's these guys who have all the money or all the girls, they glorify, you know, there's a lot of publicity around negative things. Al Capone, you know, he was glorified for being a mob king, you know, running prohibition, so he was famous for doing bad and, you know, basically for popularity. (064)

Music

The original sin started the roots of delinquency. Doing bad is not following God's way. Education and training can change these original roots of evil, potential to do bad. Also, media messages of a negative nature influence a lot of youth. Even at [a state delinquency facility], this message comes across in the music. Change most of the messages to positive. (111)

Do you think that certain types of music might affect a kid to be swayed toward delinquency?

Yes, I do. I do think some music is. I do think a lot of music is, some of the hard rock or heavy metal. I think the way they act on stage and stuff. When you go to their concerts and stuff, like the way they act, like killing rats, biting heads off and throwing them out into the crowd, and killing puppies. I think that has an effect 'cause then they get the idea that it's OK, so they'll go out and do it. And some of the rap is bad, too, 'cause they talk about 9 millimeters and stuff, so I think rap and rock have an effect on kids. (043)

City Living

I'm not saying that the city is all such a bad place, but the city is real crowded, man. If you don't got your family behind you and you don't got nobody to go to, you gotta do it for yourself, and if you live in a broken area, you know, it's even harder. You know what I'm saying? You go to school in a broken area and being constantly around violence, drugs, and abuse, no matter where you go there's nowhere for you to turn, you're still gonna be in the same area, there's nowhere for you to run away from it. (244)

. . . the city is a bad influence, you get bad things from the city. Now that [my sister's] over there with my mother she don't give my mother problems, she don't have to leave the house no more, we could do anything we want 'cause we don't have to be in danger like in the city. In the city you have to lock your house with 6 million locks on the door, you can't live in peace 'cause there's always shootouts, killings. But now like we over here by Ithaca, we can go outside, leave your car open, and when you come back it still there. Not in the city, the city was bad, that's why my mother moved. She said she didn't want to stay there anymore. When she first was gonna move, I didn't like the idea. But now that my sister's over there, she told me that it's nice. She show me pictures and I think it's nice 'cause you don't have to be in trouble with nobody around there. (012)

Getting Off Drugs

What about a kid's behavior and attitude while he is under the influence of drugs?

He don't care—what do you got to lose? Anyway, people want to go to jail so they can get off the drugs, that's what they don't realize. People want to go to jail to get off the drugs. It's not like a rehab, but they don't wanna go to a rehab. They just want to come upstate or whatever, just to get drugs out of their mind. That's what a lot of people do. When I was out there people who used to have nice clothes and stuff, everything, they just started doing drugs, started looking bad, everybody started saying, "Boy, you looking bad." They start robbing people and they get locked up. I'm happy I came up here, man. You could tell that they wanted to go to jail, you know.

A lot of kids these days, they get strung out on drugs, they realize it's really messing up their life, and the only way they can see to deal with it is to do some things that they know they're going to get sent away for.

Yes, most all the people that come upstate want to get sent here. It might sound stupid, but people want to come. But they don't do it like, "I'm gonna go snatch a chain," and then they get sent up. They plan it in a way, they try to get away with it, but they get caught and then they don't care.

So they want to help themselves, but they don't want it to look like that?

Yes. (066)

Being Good at Being Bad

How does it affect somebody if their friends are in the street and get in trouble? Is it important to be accepted into a group?

Yes, it is. When you're a younger age, like 14 or 16, it's really important to get in with the right people, prove yourself.

Even if you're with the wrong people, it's important to be with some group?

Yes, and that's why I think, you know, the reason is 'cause there's a lot of bad groups, people turn on.

Why do you think kids get involved with those bad groups?

Mainly probably 'cause bad groups are glorified.

Who glorifies it?

Other kids in school. And other reasons why they glorify them is because when they do something wrong, they say, "Well, they beat up this kid," and a lot of popularity goes to that kid in the school, maybe not all positive, but they still get some attention, and that's why they do it in groups, to get attention to make themselves better or worse.

So you think it's important to be good at something, even if it's being good at being bad, right?

Yes. (064)

CHAPTER 4

Intervention: Professional Perspectives

Our earlier presentation of professional perspectives on delinquency causation was designed to provide counterpoint to the experientially based etiological views of our delinquent cohort. For analogous reasons, the present chapter focuses on intervention—that is, the full array of prevention and remediation procedures developed and offered by the professional community: clinicians, academicians, correctional specialists, and others. Our purpose, again, is to provide a comparative basis for fully exploring the intervention perspectives and preferences of our research-partner delinquent youths.

We have chosen to define *intervention,* the focus of this chapter, as subsuming both preventive and rehabilitative activities. In this we are in accord with Martin, Sechrest, and Redner (1981), who view prevention and rehabilitation as part of a continuum rather than as discrete strategies. The commonly used distinction among primary, secondary, and tertiary prevention (Bohman, 1969) is relevant here. Primary prevention efforts are typically broadly applied interventions designed to reduce the incidence of a particular disorder or class of behaviors. Secondary prevention interventions are usually targeted to especially at-risk populations showing early signs of the condition in question. Tertiary prevention, equivalent to rehabilitation, consists of efforts to reduce the recurrence of or the impairment from conditions that already exist. All three levels of prevention—primary, secondary, and tertiary (rehabilitation)—will be our focus. However, because this is a book about, and in many ways by, adjudicated juvenile delinquents, there will be an emphasis on tertiary, rehabilitative interventions. In the terminology used by Trojanowicz and Morash (1987), our dual focus will be upon "pure prevention, which attempts to inhibit delinquency before it takes place, and rehabilitative prevention . . . which treats the youngster who has already come into contact with the formal juvenile justice system" (p. 199), with a clear emphasis on the latter.

HISTORICAL OVERVIEW

Intervention thus defined has had a roller coaster history in its juvenile corrections applications. It is a history repeatedly demonstrating that prevailing etiological conceptions of offending behavior in large measure determine the intervention strategies recommended and implemented. From the Middle Ages to the 18th century, as Martin et al. (1981) ably trace, crime was viewed as a sinful act, and humans were seen as naturally evil. It followed that reform of offenders was construed as impossible and that criminal behavior had to be countered with draconian punishments. In the 18th century, the Age of Enlightenment, thinking about the roots of human behavior in general, including offending behavior, changed drastically. Sinfulness and depravity as the energizers of human behavior were largely replaced by notions of free will and rationality, and thus the development of more humane means for encouraging behavior change became possible. Following the Civil War, a reform movement spirit crystallized in the United States and found concrete expression in the formal adoption of rehabilitation as the goal of penology by the 1870 Prison Congress in its Declaration of Principles (Henderson, 1910). Anticipating several of the core ingredients defining correctional intervention in the century that was to follow, this 1870 declaration urged indeterminate sentences coupled with rehabilitative interventions; major vocational and academic training; and transitional (back-to-community), in-community, and, especially, preventive intervention efforts.

With regard to juvenile corrections, much of this early intervention thinking was—literally—concretized in the establishment of reformatories and industrial training schools across the United States in the late 19th and early 20th centuries and, shortly thereafter, in the establishment of separate juvenile courts in almost all states "in order to protect, assist, and control rather than punish children" (Martin et al., 1981, p. 5). Coupled with this trend was heavy use of probation to permit those committing minor offenses to remain in the community. Such pro-intervention thinking—especially that promoting community-based intervention—grew in popularity as the century drew on and was given considerable further impetus by a number of influences. The 1967 report of the President's Commission on Law Enforcement and Administration of Justice strongly urged renewed emphasis on primary prevention interventions designed to change much of the economic and social character of American society. It also promoted the seeking and use of diverse means of minimizing the penetration of offenders into the (often label-creating) criminal justice system, such as decriminalization of juvenile status offenses and the total diversion from the system of those committing minor offenses.

In parallel with the primary prevention, decriminalization, and diversion interventions that then followed was a particularly widespread effort at deinstitutionalization and a companion reliance on community-based intervention. As both evidence and conviction accumulated that institution-based interventions were only infrequently effective, and as the deinstitutionalization of other populations (e.g., mentally disordered adults) became widespread in the United States, adjudicated youngsters were increasingly diverted or deincarcerated, and interventions became increasingly community based.

As we will describe more fully later in this chapter, many diverse types of community-based programs were established: halfway houses, group homes, nonresidential therapeutic communities, day treatment centers, wilderness survival programs, special classrooms, summer camps, and, for youths already incarcerated, a variety of prerelease, work release, educational release, and home furlough re-entry programs (Feldman, Caplinger, & Wodarski, 1983; Goldstein, Glick, Irwin, Pask-McCartney, & Rubama, 1989; Rutter & Giller, 1983). Community based intervention, both philosophically and operationally, became a widespread, thriving phenomenon, reflected in hundreds of separate programs nationally. But roller coasters not only rise; they also fall. Many of the evaluations of these several community-based intervention efforts conducted during the 1970s—not unlike the examinations of the effectiveness of residential treatments, whose outcome had earlier helped give rise to the community-based intervention movement—yielded negative or indeterminate results:

> Though the relevant literature is immense, most reviews have ended with essentially negative conclusions—"no delinquency prevention strategies can be definitely recommended" (Wright & Dixon, 1977); "with few and isolated exceptions the rehabilitative efforts that have been reported so far have had no appreciable effect on recidivism" (Martinson, 1974); "studies which have produced positive results have been isolated, inconsistent in their evidence, and open to so much methodological criticism that they must remain unconvincing" (Brody, 1976). (Rutter & Giller, 1983, p. 267)

Much of the intervention evaluation research of the 1960s and 1970s was of poor quality. It was characterized by a lack of appropriate controls, samples inadequate in both size and randomness of selection, poorly conceived and inconsistently implemented interventions, inadequate or inappropriate outcome measures, insufficient attention to minimizing threats to internal or external validity, use of inappropriate statistical analyses, and/or a lack of attention to follow-up measurement—a veritable rogue's gallery of experimental weaknesses.

As noted, some seized upon these experimental outcomes to conclude that "nothing works" and that the era of preventive and rehabilitative intervention should be drawn to a rapid close. Interestingly, for their own philosophical reasons, both the political left and right of the 1970s concurred and hastened the demise of intervention as a prevailing strategy. The left, on grounds of presumed infringement of the civil rights of offenders—due process, equal treatment under the law, voluntary participation and informed consent—objected to "coerced therapy to 'correc offenders as degrading, unsuccessful, and potentially repressive They urge[d] the replacement of the indeterminate sentence and the rehabilitation philosophy with a 'just deserts' philosophy of f; ed sentences based on the nature of the offense" (Martin et al., 198 . p. 6). The political right, giving expression to the justice model, called for greater use of severe punishment rather than rehabilitation and championed the goals of incapacitation, retribution, and deterrence (Vanden Haeg, 1975). Yet other objections and criticisms of rehabilitation were raised. Greenwood (1986) comments:

> The declining fortune of the rehabilitative enterprise
> has many causes: abuses of power and overreaching
> of authority by judges who attempted to impose their
> standards of acceptable childhood behavior and
> morals and by correctional authorities bent on
> improving institutional control; excessive proselytizing
> and overpromising by academic theoreticians and
> ambitious practitioners; escalating costs for treatment;
> declining sympathy for offenders; and the fact that
> rehabilitation is hard work. (p. 1)

Thus, beset by consistently negative interpretations of efficacy evaluations, subjected to attacks from both poles of the political spectrum, and targeted by a miscellany of other objections, intervention became a battered and bruised component of the juvenile justice system.

As the 1980s progressed, rehabilitation again began to find a modicum of support and encouragement, not matched by the unequivocal enthusiasm of earlier eras but support and encouragement nevertheless. First, from the several failures of the intervention effort, as well as from those that were apparently successful, came a clearer understanding of the procedural features that could lead to an effective intervention. One such constellation of features was suggested by Feldman et al. (1983):

> First, the treatment setting should be as similar as possible to the client's natural environment and, if feasible, an integral part of it . . . it is bound to minimize client reentry problems and to maximize the likelihood that learned changes will be transferred to, and stabilize within, the client's natural environment. Second, as much as possible, clients should be able to remain in their own homes. Hence, most treatment programs should not be residential ones that require a youth to live in an institution with peers who exhibit pronounced behavioral problems. Third, clients should receive maximum exposure to prosocial peers and minimum exposure to antisocial peers. Fourth, intervention programs should enable clients to perform conventional social roles and to assume maximum responsibility for their own successes or failures. Fifth, such programs should be situated in agencies that have stable financial support. (p. 34)

And Bartollas (1985) notes that "effective programs are more likely to take place when intervention is administered in humane environments, when offenders are genuinely interested in change and self-improvement in their lives, and when programs are led by dedicated staff" (p. 38). Finally, Rutter and Giller (1983) conclude:

> The two main lessons which seem to emerge from these studies are: (1) interventions need to be directed to changing the child's home environment and the patterns of parent-child interaction, and (2) in so far as the focus is on the offender himself, it needs to be concerned with improving his social

problem-solving skills and social competence
generally, rather than just seeking to suppress deviant
behavior. (p. 283)

It became clear that the sweeping conclusion "nothing works" (Martinson, 1974) was itself erroneous. Palmer (1975) showed that Martinson's singularly negative conclusion rested on his reliance on what we have called the *one-true-light assumption* (Goldstein & Stein, 1976). This assumption, the antithesis of a prescriptive viewpoint, holds that specific treatments are sufficiently powerful to override substantial individual differences and aid heterogeneous groups of youngsters. Research in all fields of intervention has shown the one-true-light assumption to be erroneous (Goldstein, 1978; Goldstein & Stein, 1976), and Palmer (1975) has shown it to be especially in error with regard to aggressive and delinquent adolescents. Palmer reviewed the data from which Martinson drew his "nothing works" conclusion and pointed out that in each of the dozens of studies concerned, there were homogeneous subsamples of adolescents for whom the given treatments under study had worked. Martinson had erred in being unresponsive to the fact that when homogeneous subsamples are combined to form a heterogeneous full sample, the various positive, negative, and no-change treatment outcome effects of the subsamples cancel each other out. The result is that the full sample appears no different than an untreated group. But when smaller, more homogeneous subsamples are examined separately, many treatments are seen to work. The task then is not to continue the futile pursuit of the so-called one true light—the one treatment that works for all—but, instead, to discern which treatments administered by which treaters work for whom.

Clearly, important beginnings have been reported in the prescription-seeking research concerned with identifying which types of delinquent youths respond and do not respond to such interventions as diversion (Gensheimer, Mayer, Gottschalk, & Davidson, 1986), probation (Sealy & Banks, 1971), individual psychotherapy (Stein & Bogin, 1978), group counseling (Warren, 1974), and behavior modification (Redner, Snellman, & Davidson, 1983). Not only have such evaluations of prescriptive efficacy emerged, but more generally positive (nonprescriptive) evidence has also been forthcoming for a number of intervention approaches—especially more recently developed behavioral and multimodal procedures (Grendreau & Ross, 1987; Goldstein et al., 1989). Awareness of such apparent efficacy has been enhanced in recent years by the contem-

porary development, and use on aggregated delinquency intervention outcome data, of meta-analytic statistical techniques (Garrett,
1985; Gensheimer et al., 1986).

The still-developing resurgence of interest in intervention has
included renewed focus not only on such tertiary prevention (i.e., rehabilitation), but also on the potential of intervention via primary
and secondary prevention. Given the conservative political climate
of the 1980s, this latter, prevention-focused interest—with its dual
emphasis on social policy change and community program
development—cannot be described as a major groundswell of correctional interest. But it is real nevertheless. One of its major features, perhaps to prove more utilitarian for preventive interventions
yet to be developed, is the substantial amount of recent research
identifying characteristics of youths-at-risk—young people for
whom preventive interventions vis-à-vis delinquent behavior are
likely to be both relevant and useful. Youngsters with such high delinquency potential often have histories characterized by (a) chronic
"acting-out" (lying, truancy, aggression, minor illegal behavior) in
childhood; (b) poor parental supervision—harsh but often inconsistent discipline practices and inadequate parental monitoring and supervision; (c) parental rejection; (d) high likelihood of parental and
grandparental criminality and alcoholism; (e) early drug use; (f) a
large number of siblings; and (g) siblings with criminal records
(Greenwood, 1986; Kazdin, 1985, 1987; Loeber & Dishion, 1983;
Morris & Braukmann, 1987). With all due caution regarding the
false positive and labeling-associated dangers of intervening with
youngsters who actuarially *might* at some future time become juvenile delinquents, it is to be hoped that such predictive information
can increasingly be put to effective use in preventive intervention.
The recent calls by Fox (1981), Lindgren (1987), Martin et al.
(1981), and others that the shared loci of such prevention efforts be
the family, the school, the workplace, and the community combine
to provide a good beginning game plan for the skilled implementation of this important intervention perspective.

We now turn to a presentation of the diverse interventions employed for delinquency reduction or prevention in modern times. As
the foregoing discussion suggests, interventions offered in actual
practice are of two broad types. Most of the interventions targeted to
youths themselves are, with a modest number of prevention-focused
exceptions, *rehabilitative* in nature. Contrariwise, most of the interventions targeted to the system of which the youth is a part (family,

school, community, etc.), with a number of rehabilitation-focused exceptions, are *preventive* in nature.

YOUTH-DIRECTED INTERVENTIONS

Youth-directed interventions primarily include judicial and administrative, setting-based, therapeutic, and several other diverse approaches.

Judicial and Administrative Approaches

Diversion

Diversion is the formal channeling of youths away from further penetration into the juvenile justice system, an early suspension of the arrest-arraignment-prosecution sequence.[1] The *diversion from* component is typically concretized by "warn and release"; the *diversion to* component, by one or another service resource for counseling, job placement, or other potentially constructive activity. In effect, the concept of diversion began with the very creation of the juvenile court system early in the 20th century as an effort to direct youths away from the several due process and correctional disadvantages that they incurred when they were dealt with in a justice system designed for adult offenders. In the decades following the creation of that system, diversion—of the warn-and-release variety—came into widespread informal use in the United States before it was recognized as a formal disposition in juvenile justice. Piliavin and Briar (1964), for example, found in one large United States city that 62 percent of adolescent offenders were released by the apprehending police following a brief lecture or reprimand. Black and Reiss (1970) and Lundman, Sykes, and Clark (1978) subsequently reported similar discretionary findings in other locations.

In the context of the long-term informal use of diversion, and in an effort to divert youths from the juvenile justice system for reasons very much analogous to those that had led to diversion from the adult justice system many years earlier, the 1967 Presidential Commission "recommended a narrowing of the juvenile court's jurisdiction over cases and supported the use of dispositional alternatives for

---

[1] Closely related or synonymous justice system programs include probation without adjudication, deferred prosecution, accelerated rehabilitative disposition, and deferred sentencing (Fox, 1981; Nietzel, 1979).

juvenile offenders that would avoid the stigma associated with formal processing, urging the establishment by Youth Service Bureaus of community-based treatment programs" (Gensheimer et al., 1986, p. 41). Thus, in its formal, post-1967 incarnation, diversion was intended to mean *treatment,* and not simply warn and release or avoidance of further processing within the criminal justice system. And indeed, the spirit and reality of diversion found fertile soil across the United States. Its endorsement and implementation spread rapidly and widely, aided in particular by funding earmarked for diversion programming under the Juvenile Justice and Delinquency Prevention Act of 1974.

A number of years have passed, and over 50 studies have been conducted evaluating the effectiveness of diversion efforts. What conclusions may be drawn? Romig (1978) reviewed eight of the previously completed diversion evaluations involving over 1,000 youths. Most were referred for individual counseling, casework, or work experience. Outcome results for diversion to these modalities were uniformly negative. Romig hypothesizes that a better outcome might have resulted had youths been diverted instead to programming centered on skills enhancement training. Gensheimer et al. (1986) conducted a meta-analysis of 44 studies designed to evaluate diversion programming efficacy. The overall conclusion was that "diversion interventions produce no effects with youths diverted from the juvenile justice system" (p. 51). Yet, as both those authors and Lundman (1984) note, diversion is no less effective than other procedures requiring further penetration of the youths into the juvenile justice system. Further, there are at least strong hints from the Gensheimer et al. meta-analysis that a more prescriptive utilization of diversion, emphasized with younger offenders, might well yield more positive outcomes—especially if greater attention were paid to the potency of the programming to which the youths were diverted. This latter suggestion gains strength from Grendreau and Ross's (1987) assertion that "the diversion literature parallels precisely the prison counseling literature, which was condemned as a failure, only to be reported later, however, that the services delivered were of abysmal quality" (p. 355).

How might diversion programming be improved? Several strong beginning answers lie in Kobrin and Klein's (1983) enumeration of the diverse concrete weaknesses of such programming to date.

1. Programs were often short term and low level and, in some settings, nonexistent.

2. Programs often were conducted in an atmosphere of turbulence and uncertainty.

3. The skill level of the program staff was often poor or highly questionable.

4. Program treatment strategy was often neither formulated nor articulated.

5. Administrative, legal, and other concerns were often given precedence over treatment considerations.

It is not just with regard to diversion, but also in connection with a number of the other rehabilitative and preventive interventions we will examine subsequently, that effectiveness will prove to be closely tied to such implementation parameters as prescriptive utilization (to whom the treatment is offered), treatment integrity (whether the treatment as described is actually delivered), and treatment intensity (concerning dose or amount and regularity of implementation).

Probation and Parole

Probation and parole are the two most common interventions used with juvenile (and adult) offenders. Both are to-the-community dispositions. Probation, used approximately six times more frequently than parole, is administered by the judicial system and has been defined as either postponing the act of sentencing an offender or pronouncing sentence but suspending its execution, with the offender's being required to meet certain conditions during a specified period of time. If the conditions are met, the sentence is not imposed (if postponed originally) or is considered served (if suspended originally). L. P. Carney (1977) reports that half of all criminal sentences in the United States take the form of probation, with its use most frequent for juvenile offenders, misdemeanants, and some categories of adult first-time felons. The use of probationary dispositions has accelerated especially rapidly in the 1980s, during which a growing attachment to "just deserts," "get tough" penological thinking has led to the widespread overcrowding of this country's jails, prisons, and juvenile residential centers.

The origins of probation are usually traced to the efforts of a British shoemaker and social reformer, John Augustus (1784–1859), who with creativity and energy was able to establish the basic procedures of probation (e.g., background investigation of candidates, supervised activities, etc.) within the British court system. Massachusetts, in 1878, became the first state to legalize the use of probation. Its use at the federal level was enacted by statute in 1925, by which time almost all of the United States had also adopted the practice. L. P. Carney (1977) suggests a number of reasons for such widespread employment of probation.

1. It maximizes the normalizing influences that are most often absent in correctional institutions but that can operate when the offender remains in the community.

2. It minimizes the psychological and physical degradations that often accompany imprisonment.

3. It is cheaper than institutional confinement, costing approximately one tenth as much as imprisonment.

4. It is (Carney holds) a more effective correctional procedure than incarceration.

As we noted earlier for diversion, the reality of the implementation of probation has proven much harsher than its promise. Caseloads are often unmanageably large; two thirds of probated offenders are seen by probation officers with caseloads over 100, though 35 is the frequently recommended maximum (President's Commission, 1967). Probationary goals far too often focus on what probationers are *not* to do and use aversive controls toward this end, with insufficient attention to the building of constructive alternative behaviors. Nietzel and Himelein (1987) capture much of what is wrong with probation in its actual operation:

> Although its personnel are poorly trained in behavioral science, they have been expected to master the social casework-medical model approach. Their caseloads are unmanageably large; their clients are often indifferent if not hostile to the entire probation concept; and they face constant demands for accountability in controlling the behavior of their charges without knowledge of what techniques to use to accomplish that control. (p. 110)

Parole has been defined as "a form of conditional release of the prisoner from the correctional institution prior to the expiration of his sentence" (Tappan, 1960, p. 709) and as "the selective and supervised release of offenders who have served a portion of their prison sentence" (Nietzel, 1979, p. 193). As with probation, the stated goals of parole are the continued rehabilitation of the offender and the continued protection of the public. Unlike probation, which is a judicial function, parole is an executive activity administered by parole boards or other correctional agencies. Parole has its roots in the late 18th and early 19th century penal policies crafted by Alexander Maconochie, governor of an early British penal colony, and the related efforts of yet another British official, Sir Walter Crofton. Maconochie (see L. P. Carney, 1977) devised and implemented a marks system in which inmates could earn their way by means of industry and good conduct through a five-phase sequence culminating in ticket-of-leave or parole (Phase 4) and total freedom (Phase 5).[2] Parole originated as a formal disposition for juvenile offenders in the United States with its use in 1825 at the New York City House of Refuge. This facility, and the several others like it that came into being, were established

> to teach juveniles how to read, write, and "cipher,"
> acquire job-related skills and, most important,
> establish habits of obedience and conformity. . . . Most
> were kept one or two years and then released under a
> procedure known as "binding out" [parole as an
> apprentice worker to adult masters]. (Lundman,
> 1984, p. 113)

The use of parole with juvenile offenders spread rapidly, continued to grow as houses of refuge metamorphosed into reform schools, and was certainly a broad and well-established disposition at both state and federal levels well before the modern era of community corrections.

Do probation and parole work? Results are mixed. Standard probation or parole supervision, across a large number of efficacy evaluations (Romig, 1978), proves every bit as effective on recidivism criteria as do a number of more expensive interventions—for example, guided group interaction, transactional analysis, psychodrama, and youth and parent lecture series. If while on probation or parole the youth is also provided certain types of behavioral intervention, such as contingency contracting, covert sensitization, and/or social skills training, he or she is likely to do better than a youth merely receiving typical case supervision (Nietzel & Himelein,

---

[2] This approach resembles in many of its particulars the levels system combined with a token economy used in a number of contemporary juvenile correctional settings.

1987). A number of negative results have been reported also. A study by the San Diego County Probation Department (1971) showed no difference between imposing probation and simply closing the case after an initial interview. A similar negative finding was obtained in independent evaluations by Empey and Erickson (1972), Feistman (1966), Kraus (1974), Pilnick (1967), and Stephenson and Scarpetti (1968). Parole has not fared much better in most formal evaluations of its efficacy, with most studies reporting no significant effects on revocation, recidivism, and similar criteria (Boston University Training Center in Youth Development, 1966; Hudson, 1973; B. M. Johnson, 1965; Pond, 1970). Yet, as with diversion, there are grounds for optimism, and they lie largely in the realm of prescriptive utilization. There is evidence that probation, for example, may yield better outcomes for adolescent offenders who are neurotic (Empey, 1969), who display a reasonable level of prosocial behavior (Garrity, 1956) or social maturity (Sealy & Banks, 1971), or who are, in the terminology of the Interpersonal Maturity System, "Cultural Conformists" (California Department of the Youth Authority, 1967). Probation appears to be a substantially less useful prescriptive intervention when the youth is nonneurotic (Empey, 1969), manipulative (Garrity, 1956), or low in social maturity (Sealy & Banks, 1971).

Probation and parole are dispositions in which offenders are either precluded from or removed from incarceration. Their effectiveness, it must be said, will be greatly enhanced to the degree that rehabilitation and correctional specialists attend with equal energy and concern to the quality of the interventions to which probationers and parolees are being removed. Matters of caseload size, probation and parole officer intervention competence, official and public commitment to rehabilitative goals, and the like will clearly determine whether probation and parole remain revolving door interventions of mixed and modest outcome or emerge as a substantially more potent means for dealing with juvenile offenders.

Setting-Based Approaches

We have explored the nature and effectiveness of a series of commonly employed judicial and administrative dispositions of delinquent youths—diversion, probation, and parole—and will shortly turn to an examination of diverse therapeutic interventions. In this section we wish to focus on youth-directed interventions defined in terms of their institutional versus community settings.

Institutional Interventions

Since the era of the houses of refuge, through the period of the reform schools and industrial training schools and continuing into the present with the use of residential youth facilities, a substantial number of offending juveniles have been incarcerated for the crimes they have committed. Quite typically, youths so treated have been multiple recidivists or, if first or second offenders, those who have committed serious felonies. Even in the 1980s, with its heavier emphasis on punishment, just deserts, retribution, and related "get tough" policies, the vast majority of offending youths receive at least one, and usually several, juvenile court dispositions of warn and release, probation, and/or community-based placement before receiving an institutional sentence. Thus, any comparisons and conclusions that might be drawn regarding the relative effectiveness of institution-based and community-based intervention must take into account such major differences in seriousness and number of offenses committed.

For the most part, institution-based interventions have not fared well over the course of a long series of efficacy evaluations. To be sure, if the outcome criterion is absence of repeat offenses, as the just deserts proponents point out, there are no such offenses during the period of incapacitation. But on other criteria—both proximal outcome indices such as institutional behavior, days spent in security, and number of assaults, and such more distal criteria as parole revocations, drug abuse, and recidivism—poor results are found for most institution-based interventions, including milieu therapy (Levinson & Kitchener, 1964), therapeutic community (Knight, 1970), self-government (Craft, Stephenson, & Granger, 1964), psychodrama (Ingram, Gerard, Quay, & Levinson, 1970), and confrontation therapy (Seckel, 1975). The reason for the repeated appearance of this outcome pattern is clearly traceable to several sources. Feldman et al. (1983) suggest that

> the factors that interfere with effective treatment in
> closed institutions are myriad and potent: they
> include severe manpower deficiencies, multiple and
> conflicting organizational goals, overpopulation and
> accompanying social control problems, prisonization,
> the emergence of negative inmate sub-cultures,
> homogenization of inmate populations, adverse
> labelling and stigmatization, inadequate generalization
> and stabilization of desired behavior changes, and

finally, excessive cost in comparison with virtually all other treatment alternatives. (p. 26)

As we will elaborate in a later section, a more recent emphasis on behavioral interventions in institutional settings has tended to yield more positive outcomes, especially regarding within-institution behavior. Here too, however, inadequacy in transfer and maintenance of gain has led to a more modest, decidedly mixed outcome on distal efficacy criteria.

In spite of this preponderance of primarily negative evaluation evidence, it is important to note in our consideration of institution-based intervention that, for philosophical reasons, and aside from concern with effectiveness for rehabilitation purposes, some are calling for the continued and perhaps increased (if differential) use of institutionalization for severe recidivists. Lundman (1984), for example, observes:

> Currently, the use of training schools and other correctional facilities for juvenile offenders is again being advocated as an effective method of controlling delinquency. Some of those urging more frequent use of training schools are incapacitation theorists. They argue that there exists a small group of repetitively delinquent offenders responsible for a large amount of youth crime . . . therefore [they] hypothesize that the solution to the youth crime problem is to sentence repeat offenders to long terms in correctional facilities. Deterrence theorists also support more frequent use of incarceration. They assert that the experience of being institutionalized alerts offenders to the painful consequences of involvement in delinquency. They also assert that punishment of particular offenders alerts other juveniles to the possibility of punishment. (p. 187)

It is indeed correct that a very small number of youths commit a very high proportion of the total delinquent offenses. Wolfgang, Figlio, and Sellin (1972), for example, found that approximately half of all offenses committed by their sample of 9,945 males in Philadelphia between their 10th and 18th birthdays were committed by but 6 percent of the cohort. A similar result was found in Columbus, Ohio, by Hamparian, Schuster, Dinitz, and Conrad (1978) and reported in their aptly named book *The Violent Few: A Study of Dangerous Juvenile*

Offenders. These findings would seem to support the aspirations of the incapacitation theorists, who hold that one need only identify such multiple-recidivists-to-be as early as possible and incarcerate them both punitively and preventively for long periods. Unfortunately, philosophical and ethical considerations aside, it is well established that our ability to predict criminal recidivistic behavior is quite poor (Monahan, 1981). Thus, Lundman (1984) appropriately comments:

> The inability to predict chronicity makes incapacitation as a general delinquency control strategy unacceptable. Early incapacitation means unnecessarily locking up too many offenders and spending too much money. Late incapacitation, waiting until chronicity is fact rather than prediction, controls too little delinquency. Incapacitation is thus a potentially effective delinquency control strategy in search of reliable methods of predicting chronicity. (p. 198)

For the present, therefore, selective incapacitation as an effective rationale for institutionalization as intervention must remain more a hope than a reality.

Community-Based Interventions

What of community-based intervention? We introduced our consideration of this approach to juvenile correction earlier, pointing out that its rise reflected the negative outcomes of the institution-based intervention evaluations just described, as well as the broader deinstitutionalization movement in the United States in the 1960s. The decline of the community-based approach began in the late 1970s as a function both of continued weaknesses in intervention implementation and evaluation and of a major rightward shift in correctional thinking in the United States away from rehabilitative or preventive programming. The hope of those championing community-based intervention was to avoid the prisonization, stigmatization, adverse labeling, and economic disadvantages associated with institutionalization and to promote effective rehabilitation. The community-based programs initiated were many and varied. Some truly reflected nothing more than the old control-oriented philosophy of many institutions simply moved to a community setting; others sought much more fully to embody intervention in, by, and with the community; most programs fell somewhere between these extremes. Some of the more noteworthy and ambitious such efforts include the San Francisco Rehabilitation Project (Northern California Service League, 1968); the Positive Action for Youth Program in Flint, Michigan (Terrance, 1971); the Attention Home Program in Boulder, Colorado (Hargardine, 1968); the Philadelphia Youth Development Day Treatment Center (Wilkins & Gottfredson, 1969); the Girls' Unity for Intensive Daytime Education in Richmond, California (Post, Hicks, & Monfort, 1968); the Essexfields Rehabilitation Project in Newark, New Jersey (Stephenson & Scarpitti, 1968); the Parkland Non-Residential Group Center in Louisville, Kentucky (Kentucky Child Welfare Research Foundation, 1967); Achievement Place teaching-family homes (Phillips, 1968); the Detroit Foster Homes Project (Merrill-Palmer Institute, 1971); the Case II Project (Cohen & Filipczak, 1971); the Associated Marine Institute in Jacksonville (Center for Studies of Crime and Delinquency, 1973); the Providence Educational Center in St. Louis (Center for Studies of Crime and Delinquency, 1973); Illinois United Delinquency Intervention Services (Goins, 1977); Project New Pride in Denver (National Institute of Law Enforcement and Criminal Justice, 1977); the Sacramento 601 Diversion Project (Romig, 1978); LaPlaya in Ponce, Puerto Rico (Woodson, 1981); the Inner City Roundtable of Youth in New York City (Center for Studies of Crime and Delinquency, 1973); the House of Umoja in Philadelphia (Woodson, 1981); and the St. Louis Experiment (Feldman et al., 1983).

We noted earlier that a great deal of the research intended to evaluate the effectiveness of community-based interventions such as these was weak in many of its characteristics. The weakness of this research is clear. What is less clear is why a strong conclusion—that such interventions do not work—should have followed from weak research. Rather, we would hold that the relevant evidence, instead of being interpreted as proving lack of effectiveness, should more parsimoniously be viewed as indeterminate, generally neither supporting nor undermining a conclusion of effectiveness or ineffectiveness. As Fagan and Hartstone (1984) observe, accepting the conclusion that nothing works is premature for at least two reasons. First, the evaluation research practices have many weaknesses, and, second, a persistent problem with many studies has been the failure to implement the intended treatment approach accurately: "If the treatment was not operationalized from theory, not delivered as prescribed, or incorrectly measured, even the strongest evaluation design will show 'no impact' " (p. 208).

As community-based intervention programs have continued to be developed, implemented, and evaluated, the beginnings of a somewhat more guardedly optimistic view may be discerned. Many programs still yield poor results, but the qualities of those that appear to work are becoming clearer. In a 1987 meta-analysis of evaluation reports on 90 community-based interventions, Gottschalk, Davidson, Mayer, and Gensheimer (1987) concluded:

> The median intervention lasted roughly 15 weeks and involved 15 hours of contact with the youths. A picture of not particularly intense interventions seemed to emerge. . . . The most popular types of interventions were some type of service brokerage, academic support or counseling, group therapy, and/or positive reinforcement. . . . Methodologically, these studies appear to have a number of problems. Few studies measured the implementation of treatment, included data collectors blind to the experimental hypotheses, or used random assignment to treatment, and no studies included random assignment of the service deliverer. In addition, over 20 percent of the studies reported some kind of unplanned variation in the treatment. Finally, 50 percent of the studies included no control group, or had a treatment-as-usual group, making it more difficult to estimate the true strength of the intervention. (pp. 276–277)

Yet these same authors also observe:

> Treatments tended to be of short duration both in terms of intensity and length. It may be that most interventions simply were not powerful enough. This last explanation seems to be supported by the data as shown by the positive correlation between ES [effect size, a standardizing index of intervention efficacy] and length of treatment. In addition, we found some evidence of experimenter effects in the positive correlation among amount of intervener and service deliverer influence and ES. . . . These findings suggest some circumstances under which community interventions with delinquents may have positive effects. If a strong treatment is used and care is taken

during the treatment to ensure that the treatment is actually being implemented as designed, then more positive effects may emerge. (p. 283)

This perspective and similar distillations of effectiveness-enhancing intervention features described earlier (Bartollas, 1985; Feldman et al., 1983) lead us to hold a "not proven, not disproven," more indeterminate, and—compared to most observers—less pessimistic perspective on this 25-year-long series of community-based intervention programs. We would assert that the following conclusions are appropriate.

1. Because essentially equivalent recidivism rates for residential and community-based interventions have consistently been reported (Bartollas, 1985; Lundman, 1984), the latter are to be preferred on grounds of humaneness and expense, except for those youths for whom the more modest supervision of probation or more severe supervision of incarceration is indicated.

2. The community intervention programs that collectively appear to be most effective are those that literally are most intense (frequent and lengthy) in delivery, best monitored to maximize correspondence between planned and actual procedures, and most community oriented—that is, most oriented toward "the reconstruction or construction of ties between the offender and the community through maintenance of family bonds, obtaining education and employment, and finding a place for the offender in the mainstream of social life" (Harlow, Weber, & Wilkins, 1971).

3. Given this emphasis on preparation for effective and satisfying within-community functioning, it appears highly desirable that community intervention for juvenile offenders include substantial stress upon acquisition of those personal, interpersonal, cognitive, and affect-associated skills that are the requisite building blocks for achieving effective family bonding, obtaining and maintaining a job, pursuing appropriate educational goals, and more generally becoming a competent, choiceful, effective individual less in need of turning to antisocial means to accomplish personal aspirations.

Therapeutic Approaches

Individual and Group Psychotherapy

One-on-one treatment (i.e., psychotherapy, counseling, case-work) has had a long history in the effort to rehabilitate delinquent youths. Healy (1915) and Aichhorn (1925) set the tone early. Both believed that delinquent behavior reflected deep personality distur-bance within the individual and that its remediation hence required in-depth individual treatment. The treatment offered was largely psychoanalytically oriented. It sought, via the establishment of a fa-vorable therapeutic relationship and the use of evocative treatment techniques, to develop insight and—it was hoped—behavior change in delinquent patients. Such work continued over the ensuing dec-ades, as a modest number of psychoanalytic and psychodynamic change agents pursued further individual treatment of delinquent youths (Crocker, 1955; Eissler, 1950; Friedlander, 1947; Gladstone, 1962; Glover, 1944; Healy & Bronner, 1936; Keith, 1984b; Ruben, 1957). As characterizes psychoanalytic work with other clinical pop-ulations, most of the foregoing efforts are single or aggregate case descriptions yielding impressionistic evidence of effect. Little faith can be placed in such data, as they are notoriously vulnerable to clin-ical bias and spurious measurement effects. Our skepticism is but-tressed by the primarily (though not totally) negative outcomes of the few evaluations of such individual treatment conducted in an investigatively more rigorous manner—for example, Adams (1959, 1961), Gutterman (1963), Jurjevich (1968), and Sowles and Gill (1970). Yet in such research, the skill of the change agent, the quality and amount of treatment actually delivered, and the presence of antitherapeutic contextual influences each subtract from the ade-quacy of the treatment offered, the evaluation of its efficacy, and our faith in the definitiveness of conclusions one can confidently draw from the evaluation of outcomes. The most appropriate stance, it would appear, is to concur with Kazdin (1985), who asserts:

> The evidence leads to one major conclusion, namely,
> the jury is still out on the effectiveness of individual
> and group psychotherapies for anti-social behavior.
> The quality of evidence is sufficiently poor to
> preclude arguing for or against the efficacy of major
> treatment techniques. (p. 102)

Group psychotherapeutic intervention for delinquent youths is of two broad types. The first resembles in history and substance the path of individual psychodynamic psychotherapy sketched previously. A medical model is applied; the youth is seen as the locus of deficits to be corrected, whereas societal contributions are largely ignored; and treatment is evocative and insight-oriented in its procedures and goals. The early work in this domain was Redl's (1945) psychodynamic group psychotherapy and Slavson's (1964) activity group psychotherapy. A substantial number of data-based studies of these interventions and their derivations have been reported, leading Romig (1978) to conclude:

> To decide whether group counseling is effective in
> the rehabilitation of juvenile delinquents, 28 studies
> involving over 1,800 youths have been reviewed. . . .
> The results of the majority of studies were that group
> counseling did not result in significant behavior
> changes. At best, group counseling allowed for the
> verbal ventilation of negative feelings of institution-
> alized delinquents. Such emotional catharsis did at
> times positively affect the youths' immediate
> institutional adjustments. However, institutional
> behavior changes did not transfer outside the
> institution. (p. 68)

The group psychotherapeutic and counseling interventions whose outcomes are reflected in this conclusion are each examples of treatment within a group—that is, the therapeutic focus is upon individual dynamics and the means for changing them within a group context. A quite different set of group intervention approaches to delinquent youths may be described as treatment by the group, in which the agents of change are other group members rather than a centralized leader. Staff members function more as facilitators and positive models than as directors, and much of the change focus is upon the individual's within-group behavior. Rather than viewing delinquent youths as "sick" and in need of "treatment," these anti-medical-model group approaches view them as responsible individuals capable of managing the group's conduct and learning to change their own behavior. This philosophy was concretized in the therapeutic community (M. Jones, 1953), guided group interaction (McCorkle, Elias, & Bixby, 1958), and the positive peer culture (Vorrath & Brendtro, 1974). These intervention approaches shared considerable popularity during the 1950s and 1960s, benefited from positive if impressionistic evidence of their value (Agee & McWilliams, 1984), and have seen declining use during the 1970s and 1980s as first behavioral treatment approaches and then antirehabilitation thinking began to figure prominently in juvenile corrections.

With regard to outcome efficacy of both individual and group treatment interventions, we have subscribed to an indeterminate, "not proven" stance. Research evaluations have yielded largely negative, though somewhat mixed, evidence of effectiveness. But research procedures have been generally inadequate; hence our "not proven" position. There is, however, an important exception to this suspended conclusion position vis-à-vis both individual and group psychotherapy for delinquent youths: the quite promising outcome evidence pattern that emerges when effectiveness data are scrutinized more segmentally and subsamples of delinquent youths are examined in an effort to determine the differential or prescriptive effectiveness of the treatment offered. We consider prescriptive intervention especially valuable in the rehabilitation of delinquents and the prevention of delinquency, and hence we wish to examine its basis and potential in greater depth here.

Prescriptive Programming

Consistently effective rehabilitative and preventive interventions are, in our view, likely to be treatments that are developed, implemented, and evaluated according to the spirit and methodology of what we have termed *prescriptive programming* (Goldstein & Glick, 1987). Simple to define in general terms but quite difficult to implement effectively, prescriptive programming recognizes that different juveniles will be responsive to different change methods. The central question in prescriptive programming with juvenile delinquents is, *Which types of youths, meeting with which types of change agents for which types of interventions will experience optimal outcomes?* This view runs counter to the prevailing one-true-light assumption underlying most intervention efforts directed toward juvenile offenders. Once again, that assumption, the antithesis of the prescriptive viewpoint, holds that specific treatments are sufficiently powerful to override substantial individual differences and aid heterogeneous groups of patients.

Both the spirit and substance of the alternative many-true-lights prescriptive programming viewpoint have their roots in analogous thinking and programming in endeavors to effect change with populations other than juvenile delinquents. Examples from work with emotionally disturbed adults and children are Kiesler's (1969) grid model matching treaters, treatments, and clients; Magaro's (1969) individualization of the psychotherapy offered and the psychotherapist offering it as a function of patient social class and premorbid personality; and our own factorial, tridifferential research schema for enhancing the development of prescriptive matches (Goldstein, 1978; Goldstein & Stein, 1976). In elementary and secondary education contexts, examples of prescriptive programming include Keller's (1966) personalized instruction; Cronbach and Snow's (1977) aptitude-treatment interactions; Hunt's (1972) matching of student conceptual level and teacher instructional style; and Klausmeier, Rossmiller, and Sailey's (1977) individually guided education model.

These ample precedents, however, are not the only demonstrations of beginning concern with prescriptive programs relevant to juvenile corrections. Early research specifically targeted to juvenile delinquents also points to the value of prescriptive programming. Several of the early findings of successful outcomes for specific interventions with subgroups of juvenile delinquents appear to be almost serendipitous side results of studies searching for overriding, one-true-light effects, a circumstance slightly diminishing their generalizability. Nonetheless, especially given our earlier, essentially negative review of their efficacy, it is worth noting the differential effectiveness of each of the two interventions most widely used with juvenile delinquents—individual and group psychotherapy.

Individual psychotherapy has been shown to be effective with highly anxious delinquent adolescents (Adams, 1962), the socially withdrawn (Stein & Bogin, 1978), those displaying at most a moderate level of psychopathic behavior (F. J. Carney, 1966; Craft et al., 1964), and those who display a set of characteristics summarized by Adams (1961) as "amenable." Adolescents who are more blatantly psychopathic, who manifest a low level of anxiety, or who are "nonamenable" in Adams's terms are appropriately viewed as poor candidates for individual psychotherapy.

Research demonstrates that a number of group intervention approaches are indeed useful for older, more sociable and person-oriented adolescents (Knight, 1970), for those who tend to be confrontation accepting (Warren, 1974), for the more neurotic-conflicted (Harrison & Mueller, 1964), and for the acting-out neurotic (California Department of the Youth Authority, 1967). Juveniles who are younger, less sociable, or more delinquent (Knight, 1969) or who are confrontation avoiding (Warren, 1974) or psychopathic (Craft et al., 1964) are less likely to benefit from group interventions. Some investigations of the efficacy of individual or group psychotherapy also report differentially positive results for such subsamples as the immature-neurotic (Jesness, 1965), those under short-term rather than long-term incarceration (Bernstein & Christiansen, 1965), the conflicted (D. Glaser, 1973), and those reacting to an adolescent growth crisis (Warren, 1974).

Other investigators, studying these and other interventions, continue to succumb to their own one-true-light beliefs and suggest or imply that their nondifferentially applied approach is an appropriate blanket prescription, useful with all delinquent subtypes. Keith (1984a, 1984b) writes in this manner as he reviews the past and current use of psychoanalytically oriented individual psychotherapy with juvenile delinquents. Still others assume an analogously broad, nonprescriptive stance toward group psychotherapy (Lavin, Trabka, & Kahn, 1984). As already noted, we strongly consider this stance to be nonproductive; evidence favoring prescriptive programming appears to us to be substantial.

In our exploration of prescriptive programming to this point, we have focused on two of the three classes of variables that combine to yield optimal prescriptions—the interventions themselves and the types of youths to whom they are directed. But optimal prescriptions should be tridifferential, specifying type of intervention by type of client by type of change agent. It is this last class of variable—the change agent—that we now wish briefly to address. Interventions, as received by the youths to whom they are directed, are never identical to the procedures specified in a textbook or treatment manual. In actual practice, the intervention specified in a manual is interpreted and implemented by the change agent and perceived and experienced by the youth. The change agent looms large in this sequence, and, just as we have all along dismissed the idea that all delinquents are equivalent, so too must we get beyond practices that treat all change agents as the same. The person who administers the intervention does make a difference. Supporting, if preliminary, evidence for this assertion exists already in the context of administering interventions to juvenile delinquents. Grant and Grant (1959) report finding internally oriented change agents to be highly effective with high-maturity offenders but detrimental to low-maturity offenders. Palmer (1973) found that change agents judged high in relationship/self-expression achieved their best results with communicative-alert, impulsive-anxious, or verbally hostile-defensive youths and did least well with dependent-anxious ones. Change agents characterized by surveillance/self-control did poorly with verbally hostile-defensive or defiant-indifferent delinquents but quite well with the dependent-anxious ones.

Agee (1979) reports similar optimal pairings. In her work, delinquents and the change agents responsible for them were each divided into expressive and instrumental subtypes. The expressive group included adolescents who were overtly vulnerable, hurting, and dependent; the instrumental group included youths who were defended against their emotions, independent, and nontrusting. Expressive staff members were defined as open in expressing their feelings and working with the feelings of others. They typically valued therapy and personal growth, which they saw as an ongoing process for themselves and for the youths they treated. Unlike the expressive delinquent youngsters, though, they had resolved significant past problems and were good role models because of their ability to establish warm, rewarding interpersonal relationships. Instrumental staff members were defined as being less comfortable with feelings than the expressive staff members were. They were more likely to be invested in getting the job done than in processing feelings and were more alert to behavioral issues. They appeared self-confident, cool, and somewhat distant. Agee thus reports evidence suggesting the outcome superiority of (a) expressive-expressive and (b) instrumental-instrumental youth/change agent pairings, a finding confirmed in substantial part in our own examination of optimal change agent empathy levels in work with delinquent youths (Edelman & Goldstein, 1984). Clearly, these several studies of youth, treater, and/or treatment differential matching are an especially promising path for future community-based intervention planning, implementation, and evaluation.

Behavior Modification

Contingency management approaches. Contingency management consists basically of two core sets of procedures. The first is designed to increase or accelerate the frequency of desirable, appropriate behaviors; it is operationalized by one or another means of delivering positive reinforcement or removing aversive stimuli (e.g., contingency contracting, token economy) contingent upon the performance of such behaviors. The second, designed to decrease or decelerate the frequency of undesirable, inappropriate behaviors, is punishment—in the form of either the removal of positive reinforcers (e.g., extinction, time-out, response cost) or the provision of aversive stimuli (e.g., reprimands; overcorrection; unpleasant tastes, sounds, odors). Both sets of procedures have been employed, often in combination, in a number of programs targeted to delinquent and chronically aggressive youths in community-based or institutional settings. Evaluations of these programs have investigated the impact of the systematic provision of diverse tangible, social, monetary, and token reinforcers (Bassett, Blanchard, & Koshland,

1975; Fo & O'Donnell, 1974, 1975; Schwitzgebel, 1967; Tyler & Brown, 1968); the use of behavioral contracting (Jesness, Allison, McCormick, Wedge, & Young, 1975); the systematic withholding or removal of such rewards via extinction (Brown & Elliott, 1965; Jones & Miller, 1974; Martin & Foxx, 1973), time-out (Bostow & Bailey, 1969; Patterson, Cobb, & Ray, 1973; White, Nielson, & Johnson, 1972), or response cost (Burchard & Barrera, 1972; Christopherson, Arnold, Hill, & Quilitch, 1972; O'Leary & Becker, 1967); and the presentation of diverse aversive stimuli, especially through means of verbal punishment techniques (Hall et al., 1971; Jones & Miller, 1974; O'Leary, Kaufman, Kass, & Drabman, 1970) or overcorrection (Foxx & Azrin, 1972; Foxx, Foxx, Jones, & Kiely, 1980; Matson, Stephens, & Horne, 1978). These are but a sampling of a considerably larger number of relevant investigations, a body of research reviewed by Grendreau and Ross (1987), Goldstein and Keller (1987), and Romig (1978). Each concludes that, as a group, contingency management procedures are regularly effective in altering a wide range of within-institution, within-community behaviors, at least for the short term. Their potency in accelerating or decelerating behavior more distal to the intervention period (e.g., in forestalling recidivism) is considerably less evident. This dual conclusion, of proximal potency and longer term weakness or, at best, indeterminacy of effect, was also drawn from two comprehensive meta-analyses of behavior modification intervention programs with delinquent youths (Garrett, 1985; Redner et al., 1983). Redner et al. (1983), also echoing our earlier call for prescriptive programming, observe:

> Yes, behavioral interventions with delinquent
> populations seem successful, particularly with
> program related and prosocial behaviors. However,
> one can neither specify optimal conditions for the
> behavioral treatment of delinquents nor claim that
> behavioral interventions are extremely successful in
> reducing recidivism for any length of time. This area
> of research has consistently omitted the experimental
> manipulation of such potentially important variables
> as the role of the change agent, participant
> characteristics, and setting characteristics, which
> would allow one to make suggestions for optimal
> intervention conditions. (p. 218)

Cognitive approaches. The several cognitive approaches to behavior modification have their theoretical roots in social learning theory (see chapter 2) and cognitive developmental theory (Gordon & Arbuthnot, 1987; Kohlberg, 1969, 1973). They are appropriately viewed as complementary in purpose to the contingency management approaches just considered. Platt and Prout (1987) comment:

> Traditional behavioral techniques applied to correctional situations have relied heavily on a conditioning model in which contingencies are manipulated in hope of changing overt performance. Cognitive-behavioral interventions would seem to support the development of an internal locus of control by having as their goal the improvement of the adoptive personal mediational processes such as self-instruction, perspective taking, and interpersonal problem solving, all of which support self-control. These approaches seek to reorient behaviorists to focus attention upon the internal processes and their influence on overt behavior. (p. 481)

As a group, the cognitive behavior modification approaches are designed to help the client both identify and correct faulty cognitions (thoughts, expectations, perceptions, beliefs) and build a repertoire of skills to deal effectively with challenging and stressful situations. Some of the approaches to the identification and correction of faulty cognitions employed with delinquent youths include self-instruction training (McCullough, Huntsinger, & Nay, 1977; Snyder & White, 1979), cognitive self-guidance (Williams & Akamatsu, 1978), thought stopping (McCullough et al., 1977), stress inoculation (Novaco, 1975), cognitive restructuring (D'Zurilla & Goldfried, 1971), perspective-taking training (Chandler, 1973), impulsivity reduction training (Camp & Bash, 1975), and moral reasoning training (Gibbs, 1986). Approaches to the enhancement of (primarily interpersonal) skills have included Interpersonal Cognitive Problem Solving (Platt & Prout, 1987), Skillstreaming (Goldstein, Sprafkin, Gershaw, & Klein, 1980), role-playing (Scarpitti, cited in Little & Kendall, 1979), modeling (Sarason & Ganzer, 1973), social skills training (Argyle, Trower, & Bryant, 1974), Life Skills Education (Adkins, 1970), and Activities for Social Development (Elardo & Cooper, 1977). Ross and Fabiano (1985) and Hollin (1989) have reviewed the efficacy evaluations of a number of these interventions. Their potency readily matches that of the contingency management behavioral approaches in short-term effectiveness and not infrequently exceeds it in long-term impact. Change in long-term out-

come, including recidivism, has not surprisingly been most pro-
nounced following implementation of intervention programs that
combine both contingency management and cognitive plus skill-
oriented components, or that are analogously multimodal (Bowman
& Auerbach, 1982; Carpenter & Sugrue, 1984; DeLange, Lanham,
& Barton, 1981; Feindler & Ecton, 1986; Feindler, Marriott, &
Iwata, 1984; Goldstein & Glick, 1987; Hollin, Huff, Clarkson, &
Edmondson, 1986).

Other Youth-Directed Approaches

Although the major intervention approaches examined thus far in
the chapter account for most of what is done to, for, and with most
delinquent youths in the United States, they far from exhaust the
programmatic alternatives. Academic educational interventions
(Ferdun, 1974; Jacobson & McGee, 1965; Reckless & Dinitz, 1972),
vocational and work programs (Hackler, 1965; O'dell, 1974; Shore
& Massimo, 1969), therapeutic camping and wilderness programs
(Kelly & Baer, 1968; Molof, 1967), positive peer culture (Vorrath &
Brendtro, 1974), guided group intervention (McCorkle et al.,
1958), reality therapy (W. Glaser, 1969), and restitution programs
(Schneider, Griffith, & Schneider, 1982) are some salient examples,
as are a few pressworthy yet questionably efficacious interventions
such as pharmacotherapeutic efforts (Campbell, Cohen, & Small,
1982; Gittleman-Klein, Spitzer, & Cantwell, 1978), shock incarceration or boot camps (A. P. Jones, 1988), and Scared Straight programs (Finckenauer, 1982). Perhaps with the exception of the latter
few, each of these alternative interventions likely deserves a place in
the array of procedures and programs that optimally will be available, for prescriptive implementation, in the difficult, multifaceted
task of reducing juvenile delinquency.

SYSTEM-DIRECTED INTERVENTIONS

Perhaps in large part because of medical model thinking, in which
delinquency is construed primarily as a disorder reflecting underlying causes existing *within* youths, most historical and contemporary
intervention approaches have been youth directed. Both political
and economic considerations, favoring attempts at immediate solutions at the lowest cost, likely abetted this tendency. Yet the delinquent youth functions within a system, both an immediate and a
broader network in which he or she grows, learns, interacts, models,
hurts, withers, thrives, and/or survives. Peers, siblings, parents,

teachers and schoolmates, employers and co-workers, codelinquents and prosocial others, and the larger community are the other actors in such real-life systems, actors who have been targeted with varying degrees of attention in system-directed interventions designed either to help rehabilitate delinquent youths or, more frequently, to prevent such offending behavior from occurring in the first place. Efforts have variously included peers, the community, the family, and the school.

Peer- and Community-Oriented Approaches

Peer-oriented programs have included the diverse programmatic efforts of Bailey, Timbers, Phillips, and Wolf (1971); Brendtro, Ness, and Nicolaou (1983); Fo and O'Donnell (1975); Furniss (1964); Litwack (1976); Patterson (1963); and Pottherst and Gabriel (1972). At the more macrolevel extreme of system-directed intervention have been those delinquency prevention/rehabilitation programs that arose largely in the heyday of sociological theories of delinquency etiology, when intervention thinking focused on correcting differential opportunity structures, differential association failures, and the like. Resultant community-level interventions included such efforts as the Chicago Area Project (Kobrin, 1959; Shaw & McKay, 1942), the Back-of-the-Yards Community Action Project (Alinsky, 1941), Mobilization for Youth (Cloward & Ohlin, 1960), The Midcity Project (Miller, 1962), Harlem Youth Opportunities Unlimited (Clark, 1965), and numerous others (see Brager & Purcell, 1967; Knapp & Polk, 1971; Marris & Rein, 1969).

Although peer- and community-oriented intervention programming is still with us, system-directed intervention efforts have in recent years come to focus increasingly on two other areas of attention and opportunity—the youth's family and the school. It is these two types of programming that we wish to examine now.

Family-Oriented Approaches

Psychodynamic Therapy

Family therapies of diverse psychodynamic, system-oriented, contingency management, and skills-training types have been utilized in the effort to prevent juvenile delinquency and to rehabilitate its perpetrators. Evaluations of intervention efficacy of psychodynamic family applications have been primarily impressionistic case reports (Curry, Wiencrot, & Koehler, 1984; F. Johnson, 1975;

Rabinowitz, 1969; Rosenthal, Moestetler, Wells, & Rolland, 1974). These reports, and the few more rigorous efforts directed at the same evaluation goals (e.g., Beal & Duckro, 1977; Everett, 1976), yield a largely "not proven" conclusion vis-à-vis such approaches to delinquency intervention. For the present, their role is and should be a modest one, perhaps finding selected and prescriptive application but substantially less use than the considerably more validated family systems, contingency management, and skills-training family approaches that we will now consider.

Family Systems Therapy

The family systems orientation is exemplified at its best in the functional family therapy approach of Alexander and his research group (Alexander, 1973; Alexander & Parsons, 1982; Barton & Alexander, 1981; Parsons & Alexander, 1973). Problematic behaviors, including delinquency, are understood in terms of the functions they serve in the family as a system and not only for the individual displaying the behavior. The dysfunctional nature of the interpersonal ebb and flow that often characterizes families of delinquent youths frequently precludes more direct or constructive fulfillment of these needed functions. Functional family therapy, therefore, seeks to change within-family communication and interaction patterns in the direction of more adequate prosocial functioning. In families of delinquent youths, targeted changes might include lowering the frequently high rate of defensiveness, increasing the low rate of mutual support, and enhancing the level of oft-absent affection. Additional goals of functional family therapy "are to increase reciprocity and positive reinforcement among family members, to establish clear communication, to help specify behaviors that family members desire from each other, to negotiate constructively, and to help identify solutions to interpersonal problems" (Kazdin, 1987, p. 81).

The treatment itself is conducted via both office-based family sessions and home-based procedures for which the family receives instruction. Evaluations of this approach have yielded consistently positive evidence of its substantial effects upon family processes and, in some instances, delinquency recidivism as well (Alexander & Parsons, 1982; Barton & Alexander, 1981).

Contingency Management

Contingency management approaches to working with dysfunctional families of delinquent, aggressive, and/or conduct-disordered youths are exemplified at their best by the parent management training program of Patterson and his group (Patterson, 1971,

1974, 1976, 1979, 1982; Patterson & Fleischman, 1979; Patterson, Reid, Jones, & Conger, 1975). Earlier in this chapter, we examined the rationale and procedures constituting *youth-directed* use of contingency management procedures to alter offending and related behaviors. Parent management training is essentially a *system-oriented* effort to train parents to function as effective contingency managers. Patterson (1982) and others have shown that parents of delinquent youths quite often function as rewarders of aggressive behavior and punishers of alternative prosocial behaviors:

> The general purpose of parent management training
> is to alter the pattern of interchanges between parent
> and child so that prosocial rather than coercive
> behavior is directly reinforced and supported within
> the family. This requires developing several different
> parenting behaviors such as establishing the rules for
> the child to follow, providing positive reinforcement
> for appropriate behavior, delivering mild forms of
> punishment to suppress (antisocial) behavior,
> negotiating compromises, and other procedures.
> (Kazdin, 1987, p. 77)

A number of investigations conducted by Patterson's group (Fleischman, 1982; Fleischman & Szykula, 1981; Patterson & Fleischman, 1979; Walter & Gilmore, 1973; Wiltz & Patterson, 1974) and by others (Forehand, Wells, & Griest, 1980; Wahler, 1980; Wahler, Leske, & Rogers, 1978) have consistently pointed to the effectiveness of parent management training in altering parenting behaviors and changing the stream of within-family functioning in less coercive, more reciprocally constructive directions, gains not infrequently maintained on follow-up.

Skills Training

Skills-training approaches to system-directed intervention for delinquent youths appear to be exemplified best by the family applications of Aggression Replacement Training conducted by our own research group (Goldstein & Glick, 1987; Goldstein et al., 1989). Aggression Replacement Training is a multimodal approach in which delinquent youths, their parents, and their siblings meet in separate weekly sessions, as often as three times a week, for training in (a) interpersonal skills, (b) anger control, and (c) moral reasoning. Through the use of modeling, behavioral rehearsal, and other social learning procedures, youths and parents are taught a 50-skill curriculum that includes negotiating, dealing with an accusation, coping with group pressure, preparing for a stressful conversation, responding to failure, expressing feelings, responding to teasing, and so forth, as well as procedures for both effectively managing their own levels of anger arousal and increasing their awareness of the needs and perspectives of other people. This approach was used with incarcerated youths, and with youths in post-incarceration, aftercare status, as well as with their families. A series of efficacy evaluations successfully demonstrated the behavior-change potency of this intervention. Perhaps most relevant to the present discussion is the study by Goldstein et al. (1989) showing significantly less recidivism when the delinquent youths, their parents, and their siblings received Aggression Replacement Training than when the youths alone received the training with no family involvement, or when no treatment was offered. Strongly suggested here is the likelihood that our most substantial and enduring outcomes may occur when the intervention provided is both youth-directed and system-directed.

School-Oriented Approaches

For purposes of rehabilitation, and even more so for prevention, schools appear to be both a convenient and a logical locus for system-directed intervention. Many school-based programs have been conducted. Filipczak, Friedman, and Reese (1979) organized and conducted the Preparation Through Responsive Educational Programs, a multifaceted intervention directed to junior high school youths and consisting of small-group instruction, social skills training, behavioral contingency contracting, and family training. Stuart, Jayaratne, and Tripoldi (1976) planned and carried out the Family and School Consultation Project, which emphasized behavioral contingency contracting between student and teacher and between student and parents. Heaton and Safer (1982) set up a school-based contingency point system with a backup reinforcement room containing tangible reinforcers and held regular meetings with parents to develop complementary home-based reinforcement patterns. Like other school-based efforts and several other kinds of youth-directed or system-directed delinquency intervention, all three of these programs yielded positive results on immediate (or proximal) outcome criteria and negative results on more long term (or distal) indices of effectiveness. Hollin (1989) summarizes this consistent pattern well:

> In summary it is possible to note a number of
> consistent findings from school-based behavioral

interventions. In the short-term the programs are, in the main, successful at improving academic performance and in ameliorating school disciplinary problems with some additional beneficial effect on family problems. However, it is doubtful whether these changes will be maintained over the long-term. There is very little, if any, evidence that school-based behavioral programs reduce the probability of future conviction for criminal behavior. (p. 147)

We do not disagree with Hollin's conclusion. However, we would add our belief that such interventions do have the potential for at least contributing to a long-term, positive outcome of reduced or eliminated offending behavior when they are not only—as we have urged for all types of interventions—prescriptively and intensively offered with integrity to procedural plan, but also multimodal in substance. We have illustrated the notion of multimodal intervention in our earlier discussion of Aggression Replacement Training employed as a family-targeted approach (Goldstein et al., 1989). We now wish to illustrate this perspective further, this time in the context of school-based intervention.

Goldstein, Apter, and Harootunian (1984) have compiled a listing of over 100 interventions reported in the literature as attempted solutions to school violence and vandalism in the United States. As Table 2 indicates, such efforts may have as their focus the students themselves, the teachers, the curriculum, the school administration or governance, alterations in physical aspects of the school environment, parents, security personnel, the community of which the school is a part, and the larger state or federal context. To illustrate the multimodal intervention perspective that we wish to champion as potentially highly productive, we have selected 20 of the interventions listed in Table 2 and recast them in a level-by-mode matrix in Table 3.[3] Specifically, the 20 interventions are arranged in rows by the levels of community, school, teacher, and student as their intended targets, and in columns by modality as psychological, educational, administrative, legal, or physical in substance. Thus, interpersonal skills training is a student-oriented, psychological intervention; an adopt-a-school program is a community-oriented, administrative

---

[3] The 20 interventions were chosen to illustrate the multimodal theme, not because they are necessarily more potent than any of the others in Table 2.

intervention; and so forth. Because we believe strongly that juvenile delinquency and such often accompanying behaviors as chronic aggressiveness, diverse school-associated difficulties, and the like are themselves of multilevel origin, their rehabilitation and prevention are likely to be most rapidly and enduringly enhanced if corrective efforts applied are correspondingly complex multilevel, multimodal interventions.

TABLE 2 Attempted Solutions to School Violence and Vandalism

STUDENT ORIENTED

Diagnostic learning centers
Regional occupational centers
Part-time programs
Academic support services
Group counseling
Student advisory committees
Student patrols (interracial)
Behavior modification: contingency management
Behavior modification: time-out
Behavior modification: response cost
Behavior modification: contracting
Financial accountability
School transfer .
Interpersonal skills training
Problem-solving training
Moral education
Values clarification
Individual counseling
More achievable reward criteria
Identification cards
Peer counseling
Participation in grievance resolution
Security advisory councils
School-safety committees

TEACHER ORIENTED

Aggression management training for teachers
Increased teacher-student nonclass contact
Teacher-student-administration group discussions
Low teacher-pupil ratio
Firm, fair, consistent teacher discipline
Self-defense training
Carrying of weapons by teachers

Note. From *School Violence* (pp. 12–13) by A. P. Goldstein, S. J. Apter, &
B. Harootunian, 1984, Englewood Cliffs, NJ: Prentice-Hall. Copyright 1984 by Prentice-Hall, Inc. Reprinted by permission.

TABLE 2 *(cont'd)*

TEACHER ORIENTED (cont'd)

Legalization of teacher use of force
Compensation for aggression-related expenses
Individualized teaching strategies
Enhanced teacher knowledge of student ethnic milieu
Increased teacher-parent interaction

CURRICULAR

Art and music courses
Law courses
Police courses
Courses dealing with practical aspects of adult life
Prescriptively tailored course sequences
Work-study programs
Equivalency diplomas
Schools without walls
Schools within schools
Learning centers (magnet schools, educational parks)
Continuation centers (street academies, evening high schools)
Minischools
Self-paced instruction
Idiographic grading

ADMINISTRATIVE

Use of skilled conflict negotiators
Twenty-four-hour custodial service
Clear lines of responsibility and authority among administrators
School safety committees
School administration-police coordination
Legal rights handbooks
School procedures manuals
Written codes of rights and responsibilities
Aggression management training for administrators
Democratized school governance
Human relations courses
Effective intelligence network
Principal visibility and availability
Relaxation of arbitrary rules (regarding smoking, dressing, absences, etc.)

PHYSICAL SCHOOL ALTERATIONS

Extensive lighting program
Blackout of all lighting
Reduction of school size
Reduction of class size
Closing off of isolated areas
Increase in staff supervision
Rapid repair of vandalism targets
Electronic monitoring for weapons detection
Safety corridors (school to street)
Removal of tempting vandalism targets
Recessed fixtures where possible
Installation of graffiti boards
Encouragement of student-drawn murals
Lockers painted bright colors
Use of ceramic-type, hard surface paints
Clean-up, pick-up, fix-up days
Paving or asphalting of graveled parking areas
Plexiglass or polycarbonate windows
Decorative grillwork over windows
Identification marking on all school property
Personal alarm systems
Use of intruder detectors (microwave, ultrasonic, infrared,
    audio, video, mechanical)

PARENT ORIENTED

Telephone campaigns to encourage PTA attendance
Antitruancy committees (parent, counselor, student)
Parenting skills training
Parents as guest speakers
Parents as apprenticeship resources
Parents as work study contacts
Increased parent legal responsibility for children's
    behavior
Family education centers

SECURITY ORIENTED

Police K-9 patrol units
Police helicopter surveillance
Use of security personnel for patrol

TABLE 2 *(cont'd)*

SECURITY ORIENTED (cont'd)

Use of security personnel for crowd control
Use of security personnel for intelligence gathering
Use of security personnel for record keeping
Use of security personnel for teaching (e.g., law)
Use of security personnel for counseling
Use of security personnel for home visits
Development of school security manuals

COMMUNITY ORIENTED

Helping hand programs
Restitution programs
Adopt-a-school programs
Vandalism prevention education
Mass media publication of costs of vandalism
Opening of school to community use after hours
Improved school-juvenile court liaison
Family back-to-school week
Neighborhood days
Vandalism watch on or near school grounds via mobile unit
Reporting by CB users of observed vandalism
Community education programs
More and better programs for disruptive or disturbed youngsters

STATE AND FEDERALLY ORIENTED

Uniform violence and vandalism reporting system
State antiviolence advisory committee
Stronger gun control legislation
Enhanced national moral leadership
Better coordination among relevant federal, state, community
    agencies
Stronger antitrespass legislation
More prosocial television programs
Less restrictive child labor laws

TABLE 3 A Multidimensional Intervention Strategy for School Violence

MULTILEVEL TARGETS OF INTERVENTION	MULTIMODAL INTERVENTIONS					
	Psychological	Educational	Administrative	Legal	Physical
Community	Programs for disturbed children	Prosocial television programs	Adopt-a-school programs	Gun control legislation	Near school, mobile unit vandalism watch
School	Use of skilled conflict negotiators	Prescriptively tailored course sequences	Reduction of class size	Legal rights handbooks	Lighting, painting, paving programs
Teacher	Aggression management training	Enhanced knowledge of student ethnic milieu	Low teacher-pupil ratio	Legalization of teacher use of force	Personal alarm systems
Student	Interpersonal skills training	Moral education	School transfer	Use of security personnel	Student murals, graffiti boards

CHAPTER 5

Intervention:
Youth Perspectives

What do *you* think could be done to prevent or reduce juvenile delinquency?

As was true for the youths' etiological thinking, their suggestions for delinquency prevention and reduction were often creative in concept and articulately framed. Some were quite novel; others were readily predictable. As professionals who report the intergenerational transmission of physical abuse often suggest, harshness of experience appears to breed harshness of response. The single most common youth-suggested set of interventions urged *punishment*, often quite severe punishment. Consistent with and following from their heavy etiological emphasis upon dysfunctional parenting as a major cause of delinquency, many respondents urged training in *parenting* and enhanced parent-youth communication as potentially significant prevention/reduction interventions. A small array of *counseling* approaches, a wide array of suggestions relating to *recreation,* and a number of proposals associated with the *schools* were also put forth by our project participants. Like their perspectives on causation, several youths proposed *multicomponent interventions*—some fanciful, others of seemingly applied relevance to the real world of delinquency intervention. Finally, a large number of *miscellaneous* suggestions, very diverse in content and often unusually novel, were also provided.

The excerpts presented here are a sample of youth-offered "ordinary knowledge" selected from our study's 250 interviews on the basis of representativeness, clarity, and collective range of youth perspectives. Throughout the chapter, the interviewers' questions are indicated by italic type. The numbers at the end of each portion of interview material identify the various respondents.

PUNISHMENT

Incarceration Alternatives

Incarceration

What is your opinion on what would be an effective way of preventing juvenile delinquency in America?

Well, my way would be to catch them, you know, sentence them. Give them some time to let them know what it feels like to be locked up. And let them know what it feels like to be away from your family, your girlfriend, you know, people you love. (049)

Harsher Incarceration

Yeah, they should do that because sometimes they start hanging outside and they could get locked up for nothing, and when they send a kid upstate they should not send them to a little playhouse because that's like milk and cookies, you know. They're going to be like, yeah, let me go upstate because they serve me nice food. They should send them to a place where they would never want to go back.

Are you saying that—when they go upstate, do you mean DFY [Division for Youth], some of the DFY facilities upstate?

Yeah, it's too easy. (087)

I think the judges should get a little bit harsher. If kids commit crimes they should pay for it. Even if it's like petty theft, you should get like 2 years probation at least. Now they only give them like 6 months, that don't even make the kid think about it. And when it's your second offense double their time, and if they make a third offense put them in a reformatory, detention, or a home of some sort. Not like now, because now they wait until you commit like 70 crimes and then they finally put you in there, and when they do it's like 16 months. They should double everything, even their time. (091)

Well, if I were the director of [the state delinquency facility], in a way not to try to harm them or hurt them, nothing like that, I'd try to make their time hard and rougher on them. To make their stay . . . more rough on them so when they leave . . . you know, they could pass it on how their time was when they was here. 'Cause to the younger brothers that is coming up, they could pass it on to them.

So you were saying, if you were the director and you could make the decisions, what do you need to do to help kids in a facility not to get in problems, not to get involved? You said get a little tough on them. How are you going to get tough on them? What are you going to do?

You know, like when they be here, like I say when I first came here, you know, I had a few problems. But being that I was getting yelled at a lot, there's some things that I learned from when I was getting yelled at, some things that I picked up on. When they get back to, you know, you making their time here more miserable. I think when they get back out I think they'll think twice before they do something, you know, and try to get locked up again 'cause they won't think it's like a toy, you know, that they can just go out there and do this and they gonna come and they gonna get locked up and they gonna be just like they was on the outside, like when they was home with their mother, whatever they wanted, they got it. (057)

To tell you the truth, I think placements now, the homes and stuff, I think they're treating kids too good. I think they have to treat them—treat them with respect, but like you're giving them too much, too much freedom, and you know that's what they want. Like you're up there and you're happy. It's like a camp, like you're just going away to a summer camp. They get to go off grounds like to movies. Even if their behavior is good, give them something else but give them on grounds. It's like they're living too good.

Are you talking specifically about DFY programs?

Yeah.

You know DFY programs, don't you?

Yeah.

You're saying that the kids in DFY programs are having too good a life, and you're suggesting in order to reduce the delinquency behavior, then we should not give kids such a good life.

Yeah, make it tougher for them.

Make them suffer, you're saying?

I think so, because once they leave, they like say, "Well, it's not bad up there, so it doesn't matter if I get caught. I get three hot meals and a cot," you know, "three hot meals a day and a bed to sleep in." So they really don't mind. And then for the people who don't care about their family, forget it. They living up there, they got people who care for them, and then they got clothes. They give them a lot of things, and I think if you would take some of the privileges away from them, I think they would think twice.

Yes, that's a good idea. Are you giving that as an answer for reducing [delinquency], or do you think that would also prevent youngsters from doing this in the future?

Yes, 'cause what stopped me is I know my next stop isn't DFY, it's going to be jail, and I don't want to go there—I heard that it's tough. Now if the younger kids hear that DFY is getting tougher, then they'll think twice. (085)

Mandatory Incarceration

The devil just got their mind completely, you just can't tell them nothin'. He just has their mind under control, and so the only way you going to stop them is have the police get them and go in front of the judge. Judge say 5 years mandatory, you go to jail and that's that. I know he gotta think, 'cause some days when he in there beaten on or watching somebody else, he gotta think. (001)

Sentencing of Youths as Adults

Now in terms of what you've said, how do you think society can prevent young people from doing the things they do?

By punishing them real bad, like don't play with them. Once they do a crime they should sentence them. They should not let the people have hearings because that's not right because they know they committed a crime. They should have curfews—they should have jobs.

You mean in the homes, you're saying. Once they have committed the crime and gone to court, court should deal with it almost like an adult?

Mostly like an adult, not like a child, because if it's a child they're going to keep doing it. If they do it like an adult, if they get sentenced like an adult, they won't play no more. (087)

Longer Incarceration

What kinds of things do you think they should do different?

Restrict them. Not release them until they are totally sure. Make it a longer period of time. Longer before home visits. I am going to get murdered someday for this. (111)

Life Sentences

If you were made the mayor of your city and someone said to you, "We'll give you anything you need to stop delinquency in your city," what would you do?

For one thing, I would have all the cops go through each place and see if they have drugs, and just wipe them right out. Take them to prison and keep them there for life. And for all the kids that's doing wrong, I would think that they would need some great counseling. They would need probation for at least 1 year, and if they don't make probation they just gonna have to go to a home or a place like this until they get right. (006)

Life Sentences Without Food

What about the sexual abuse issue?

I think that when that happens they should put the person in jail forever. I mean if I was the mayor, I would lock 'em up. I would not feed them or anything. I would let them go hungry. I'm serious. Because that's not right for anyone to go through. (006)

Incarceration of Parents

Also possible, if parents were held more accountable, then the parents would be more strict. If the parents got arrested for what the child did, maybe the parents would watch them more closely. If parents act like they don't care, the chances are the kid will get into trouble. If they are strict up until age 15, then maybe the kid would do better. (202)

Incarceration With Attack Dog

Every person they catch with a drug . . .

What do you think they ought to do?

They should take 'em down to the police station and just sit 'em in the dark. You know, the cages they sleep in, the police put you in when you go down there?

Yeah.

Just tell 'em to sit in there until you tell me the truth and until I think you've stopped. Then they goin' to put a dog in there and just tell 'em to sit. You know, the dog goin' be trained, and if you even make the wrong move, mess with the handcuffs too much, he goin' attack you.

So you're saying that if you scare kids, they will not return to a life of crime.

Uh-uh, some. I saying this for some kids, not for all.

So for some kids a program like this will work?

Yep.

And for other kids you just have to really be hard with them?

Don't give them no slack. (001)

Other Punishments

Stricter Parents and Schools

What could parents do to help?

Be stricter. That's the main thing, strict from birth till—until adult.

How about schools?

I think schools should be stricter, too. I think that in school you shouldn't be allowed to go out from school. At some schools they let you go out for lunch and something. You should eat lunch inside, have a little courtyard inside the school, but I don't think they should go outside. They should be real strict. (034)

Involuntary Drug Rehabilitation

It should be a law that if a kid gets picked up for being under the influence of drugs that he go to a drug rehab center. Maybe if they dealt with the problem when it first happened, it would prevent people from being burnouts. (111)

Scared Straight Programs, Other Demonstrations

I say the best thing you could do is just like let them talk to people who are going through or having the same problems that they are having. Let them know what that person experiences, because I see now like a lot of little kids say jail is so awful but they don't really know until they went there. The school took me up to Sing Sing Prison, and I ain't going to lie, I got kind of scared in there because the men, they would have beat you up and not cared because they're already there for life, so they have nothing to lose. (107)

Show them movies, like horror movies, blood movies, like in drivers' ed. Stuff like that that happens in reformatories and stuff like that, 'cause I wouldn't go to a reformatory. (117)

How can we get a message out there to kids so that before they got involved in that cycle they would know what the story was going to be and they could say, "No, I don't want any part of that, my life's together and I don't want to end up dead or in jail"?

Make some type of movie or something, show some type of movie. You get a movie like that about a drug dealer, show them the real life, when a kid first gets hooked.

So you show a young boy, 9 or 10 years old, when he first starts getting attracted to that stuff, the money, cars, and clothes, and show him getting hooked up with a dealer and then show all the other stuff, the stuff that isn't so glamorous, people knocking on doors in the middle of the night and demanding drugs or money.

And when he starts seeing stuff like people dying—pow, pow—he'll be scared. You see one of your good friends die, that's when I guarantee you leave drugs or whatever alone. That's when you leave it all alone. Stupid stuff, man. (066)

Curfew

Well, in your opinion, what can be done out there? What do you think would help kids?

Probably curfews at night. Try to make sure—have a certain age on what you can do and what you can't. (053)

More Gun Use

I would like to legalize like guns and stuff so all the store owners could have guns and stuff. Like have a permit for store owners or something. I say like if one kid gets shot walking in a store trying to rip off something, then the second kid ain't going to be dumb enough to try it. And when that starts happening all over the United States, people getting hurt from doing stupid shit, I think everybody would start getting scared of doing it. (091)

House Arrest by Parents

If you were in charge, what could you do to stop them?

I don't think you can. If it was my child and I found out he was stealing or whatever the case may be, I would ground him, keep him in the house. If he's like 17 or 18, he knows what will happen if he gets caught—he'll go to jail. If he's under 16, I would keep him in the house no matter what the cost.

Could anyone have kept you in the house?

Yeah.

You talk about peer pressure and what parents should do, and it's right at the time when you want parents' attention and you also want some freedom, and it's a hard time to balance.

Yeah, but if they just understand that the only reason the parents are keeping you in the house is for your own good, then they shouldn't mind it. You see, what I'm saying, the kids shouldn't mind it if the parents keep them in the house. If the parent goes to the grandmother's house, then the kid could go with her, but not on their own, because he'll probably get in trouble. (050)

PARENTING

Parent Training

What would you do to help families?

Families with problems? Well, I would have these places open for parent training. Like how they have here, where we come and learn and stuff. Have one where the parent can go. Well, we not saying you not a good mother or nothin', maybe you trying, maybe you don't know how to go about it, so now we gonna teach you. Parents that was willing to come and learn would probably feel better about themselves, which would be good. Have a place like this for grandmothers and how they could change theyselves too. But they don't have places like that. And I'd have a few places like that. (008)

But what if the parents don't know how to do all that stuff?

Well, if the parents don't know how to do it, I think when they have a child maybe they can go to special people, like maybe a therapist, so that way they can express their feelings and that way the therapist can help them find different ways like, well, if you have problems and think that way, maybe you can come see us or you can write your feelings down. Maybe go on walks, go to parenting things, like go there and find out what you got to do, because if you don't know what to do, then you might be abusing your child. (002)

Do you think your parents have anything to do with you getting involved in juvenile delinquency?

Yeah, somewhat. They're not consistent enough. I mean, they have limited parenting skills.

What do you think would prevent that from happening?

They should get counseling, and that way they'd become a better parent. They should learn what punishments are appropriate and they should be consistent. (079)

There ought to be classes for parents . . . to teach them how to recognize the early signs of a kid headed for trouble. Most parents don't recognize the beginning signs until it's too late. (054)

Parent-Youth Communication

What about—what could anyone do to prevent [delinquency]?

To prevent it, I think that if they talked to their parents a lot and expressed how they're really feeling about school. If they are getting pressured, to come home and talk to their parents and let their parents know, "Hey, I was tempted into doing something delinquent today. What should I do?" Maybe they could even go to some type of family counseling or something with their families. Maybe that would help them out a lot. (014)

Well, if that's what causes delinquency, what can anyone do to prevent delinquency?

Try to look for a positive friend, try to look for positive friends that will influence them into positive things. And when they see their mother do bad things, just try to talk to their mother about it. Try to talk them out of doing a negative thing. (017)

If I was a parent and my kid wanted to do something, and I didn't want them to do it, I would sit them down and explain to them why I didn't want them to do it. Like drugs—if they came out and said, "I want to try drugs," I may be upset but I wouldn't yell at them. I'd sit them down and explain to them that drugs are bad for you and tell them all the dangers that drugs can do to you, and tell them that I care about you and all this and everything. And just tell them how I feel and then listen to how they feel about it and try to give them other things they can think about doing instead of drugs. (095)

Do you feel kids need explanations?

Yeah, parents will tell their kids, "Don't do this because I said so"—they don't tell their kids the reasons. Like don't do drugs because they're bad for you, read to them about it, get movies about it, show them what happens when they're still 8 and 9 years old. Don't wait until they're 15.

Start young?

I'm serious, when I was 13 in '85 I started doing drugs. That was young to do drugs. Little do people know that my sister started the same time I did, and she's only going to be 14 now. She was like 10 at the time. I see little kids, 7- and 8-year-olds, popping pills, shooting up, smoking. My sister is 7 now. When she was in kindergarten she was skipping school, and none of my sisters are virgins, even the 7-year-old. Now talk about a pretty rowdy family—I can honestly say only the 2-year-old is a virgin. (093)

How do you think the world could prevent delinquency?

When they raising up they kids, tell about these type of things, 'cause if you don't tell your kid about somethin' and they be in school one day and they friend go, "Come here, let's do this," they do it. Nobody ever told them not to do it. So therefore they might get involved just by not knowing. So I think once my kid get 13 I will sit her down—or maybe younger—and just say, "This is things you gotta know." Drugs, I mean if I had to show them each little thing and go into detail like a classroom thing, I would just do it. And first you gotta have a relationship with your kid where they listen to you—anyway, you know what I'm saying. Then when you talk to your kids they listen to you, and when you tell them stuff and show 'em and then they know about it, like you could say, "Don't mess with any type of guys" or somethin' like that. Tell them about drugs, so when they get hit in the face with it they gonna know about it and say no or stuff like that. I think if more parents do that, at least 40 or 50 percent would get better. 'Cause a lot of parents, they don't even tell their kids nothin' . They feed and bring 'em up, like letting them make all the decisions theyselves. And then half the time the parents are doin' it . . . so first you have to be a good parent by doing things that you want your kid to do. Like if you want your kid to go to school, you go to school first. I heard on the radio this morning "My big brother told me, 'Don't do drugs,' but he OD off it." I'm not gonna want to listen to nobody who beating people up tellin' me not to fight, so you gotta like set a good role model for the person you want to help. (008)

Other Parenting-Associated Interventions

Stricter Parenting

OK, can you think of any ways that we could reduce delinquency or keep kids out of trouble with the law?

Well, I think a lot of it would have to do with the parents. Parents would really have to like put their foot down and be a lot more stricter than they are now. Now, like kids are gettin' away with anything. They parents just have to be more strict and lay down the rules and really go by the rules and not slack up on them. (007)

OK, why do you think that juvenile delinquency happens, and what could we do to prevent it?

Parents should know where their kids are all the time. Even when they don't want to tell you. If there is a party, you should let your kid go, but just warn them ahead of time and set the guidelines and be strict about it. Tell them they should take you seriously if there is going to be drugs and alcohol there. Still let them go. Just encourage them not to do drugs and drink. Set guidelines for them, what time they should be in and stuff. If they miss it a lot, just ground them or do something so they know you aren't going to take it, because they are going to keep trying to see how much they can get away with. It is just going to lead to bigger and more problems. (152)

Early Discipline

Well, first of all, they should have started to discipline me when I was younger. They should have started that a long time ago. I don't know, maybe it would have helped and maybe it wouldn't have. Sometimes when you do something your parents tell you not to do and you do it anyways, and sometimes you want your parents to tell you, you want them to discipline you, 'cause that's how I feel sometimes. Sometimes I feel that way, like they should really try to get down on being disciplined. (081)

Early Adoption for Unwanted Children

What would you do with the parents?

I would find a way to help parents work on their children more—if they don't want them, as soon as they are born have them adopted or something so they are wanted. Or don't spoil the kid so much that he gets away with everything, but don't push him away so much that you don't really care about him so much. If you're going to care about him it's all right, but if you're not, have him adopted or something, 'cause there's no sense in having and destroying him because you don't want him. You should never spoil a kid—that's the worst thing you can do to him. (091)

Parental Love

OK, so a reliable home. What goes into making that home reliable so that the child is going to feel secure there?

The child definitely needs to feel loved by the parents, and the parents need to let the child know that they are going to be there for the child through thick and thin. I think that a child definitely needs to know that he has somebody in the world because it's like throughout the child's life, if he don't have nobody, that's where a lot of trouble is going to start, and it could make that child become a juvenile delinquent. (163)

Values Training

I want to say the environment because I have a kid that lives in my building right across the hall from me on the second floor, he's about 17, he been living there for about 8 years, he came there when I came there. You see, this kid, he'll go to school, he got a job, you know, he go to parties with me and my brother sometimes, he hang with us, you know, it's just that he was brought up and he knew right from wrong and he knew—he proved to his mother that he wasn't gonna get in trouble. Now this kid is 17 going on 18. He's been around places where people are shooting and all that, but this kid hasn't fallen into that category as other kids are, so you can't really blame it on the environment.

Why is it?

Because his mother taught him right from wrong and he know right from wrong. He knew what to do out there and what not to do. (237)

COUNSELING

Nonspecific Suggestions

OK, what types of things do you feel can be done to help out the juvenile delinquents? What I'm thinking about is in the community. Are there things that can take place in the community that can help the kid that is in trouble?

Yes, you could ask for help. You could go to a psychiatrist or a drug rehabilitation program like AA meetings. Just ask for some good advice from other people older than you, like grandparents or something. Just people that know what's right and wrong, 'cause you don't exactly know the good things or the bad things quite yet. Or you do, but you don't want to quit them because of your peers. (053)

You know, when kids hold a lot of things inside, it causes kids to do a lot of bad things. And I held in a lot of things inside of me, myself. And I had a lot of problems, too, and I'm just now starting to work on my problems. I wasn't given a lot of attention that I wanted and that was in my family home, and when you're not given a lot of attention and you feel bad about yourself, and I was miserable and that caused a lot of my problems. I think that's something that teenagers need help with. If they have problems, give them some kind of counseling, help them to realize that it's not their fault, their problems. (038)

I think with me that counseling never helped. My DFY worker sent me to all kinds of counselors. I hated them. They don't want to help me. Like a program like this. You have staff that really want to help you. But then again I see some staff that just work to overpower us. Counselors, you know they are getting paid whether you're getting helped or not. Their life is going to go on. They are just doing it because they are getting paid for it. I don't think that helps at all. I think if somebody were to come on their own free time and just talk with you and just do things with you and gradually try and talk to you and share some of their experiences with you. And make you feel that you are not obligated to tell them. (016)

Can you think of anything else anyone could do to make the problem of delinquency better, to help kids stay out of trouble?

Maybe they could have built up a place like to have people have self-esteem. Delinquent kids, they get in trouble in the end, and people that have low self-esteem get together on certain days and talk about their problems they had during the week, and once they talk out their problems they would probably feel better. (017)

Family Counseling

What could the schools do?

Yes, the schools could send people to talk to the family together, like a psychiatrist or something, like somebody just to talk to, to get the whole family together and just sit there and talk. (044)

Peer Counseling

You've covered two areas. What about facilities? What do you feel can be done to help juvenile delinquents involved in problems in facilities?

I think that the counseling is the most important part—make sure they get the one-on-one counseling. You know, which might really help them, or even peers because I feel delinquents with problems, I think, find it easier to talk to a peer than an adult. Because peers know what you are talking about, and they've gone through it, and they know things to do like might help you to solve these problems, especially if they have the same problems. The adults, some of them have problems, but most of the adults, they really don't know exactly. They haven't felt what we were feeling. What it is to be locked up or away from home for a certain amount of time because they always go home at night and they ain't got to worry about it. (060)

Any other kinds of programs that you know of or that maybe would have helped you?

There's one program that I went to that did help me. It did actually help me. It was a counselor session that I used to go to to deal with problems in the family and with peer pressure. It helped me a lot because the way they had it, it wasn't like you were sitting there with just a whole bunch of adults around. You had kids your own age that went through similar problems, and you discussed them openly, got advice on them and what you should do, and we did some worksheets and stuff on what kids should do when a problem arises in the family and stuff and who they should talk to and who would be the best person to talk to when they have that problem, and we also learned how to talk to your parents about problems.

That sounds good. So this was like a peer group counseling?

Yep. (087)

Intensified Probation Counseling

So what can people do to help someone change from what they've become?

Work with him, try to get it through to him that he should not commit a crime. Try to get it through to him that it's not worth going to jail for 5, 6 years. Try to influence him that he just wasting 5 precious years of his life. You gotta just keep on working with him. You've gotta really influence this person to do these things, you know, like he *has* to do it . . .

You're saying, basically, don't give up?

Right. What I really think, you know, that when someone commits a crime they don't work with them. Like probation. Some might get put on probation. They come and say, "OK, how's your day? Oh, it was good—OK, sign the sheet." They sign it, then they leave. That's not working with anybody. That's not teaching them nothing. So you see a probation officer for a year, what's that gonna do? Nothing. That's how it is. Like when a probation officer—when you have to see a probation officer they should keep them there for like 2 or 3 hours. Keep talking with him. Ask him what he feels, what did he do wrong, what good things did he do this week, all this stuff. Then maybe they can get ideas to help him. Keep checking up on him, like if he's supposed to be in the house at a certain time, see if he's there. (249)

Aggression Replacement Training

Are there things kids learn in a facility that are really useful to them and that would help them after release?

If it's a place like this, I know a lot of kids leave here. I know I'm going to leave here with a lot of things I didn't know before.

People do learn a lot of stuff, like the anger control, the skills, and the moral reasoning. Basically everything that they learn here they can use out in the world in some way. Maybe not in every situation they might not be able to use it, but most situations they can—a better way to handle themselves. (047)

RECREATION

Videogames, Sports

They should have some after school activities, like videogames and basketball. This would keep kids busy and keep them off the street. (023)

Parks, Concerts, Arcades

I was bored, so I had nothing to do. They could have more parks or something like that or more amusement things. More better places to hang out. More things to do. To be specific, more concerts or arcades, things local, like around the vicinity of where you live, or more malls. Or other things like hanging out for summertime. People would like to go swimming. (161)

Hobbies, Drama

Try to help you, like keep you busy, occupied, help you do things, like what's your hobbies, and then help you with your hobbies and you don't need to be delinquent. And in school do programs, drama, stuff like that. (012)

Gymnastics

They could do like I said, they could go help them, they could do it every day like that . . . stuff, cause I know like around my house they made this special program for kids to do gymnastics and judo, and a lot of kids stay out of trouble from that. And it's like a special program, and they help them. (012)

Recreation Centers

I feel that there should be more, you know, like you know, centers and stuff. Most of the centers are on the east side and south side—there are none on the, you know, _____. (012)

Neighborhood Clubs

Something they could do would be to have some type of neighborhood club or "hangout" houses. Kids could go there and be accepted for what they are. There would have to be counselors there to talk with and try to help them. Since there would only be kids there who wanted to make some changes, then they wouldn't have all the pressure and embarrassment from trying to do something good. (101)

Arcades

If you were in charge of the juvenile justice system and you wanted to help kids, what would you do? What would you do to help the kids, and what would you do to help prevent kids from getting in trouble?

I would probably talk to somebody to like open up more arcades, because that seems to keep a lot of kids out of trouble. And probably build something to keep the kids active instead of thinking about getting in trouble all the time. So I would build something to keep the kids occupied in each town. (097)

YMCAs

Of all of these reasons you said cause delinquency, I think . . . some of those things have changed. You said it was family things, community things, and peers and stuff like that. Those things haven't changed. How are you going to be good when you go back there?

Well, I plan to keep myself more occupied and to stay away from my friends to keep myself out of trouble. Like when I went on my home visit, my aunt and I started lookin' around for a Y that I can join. And when I go to school, from that I'll go straight to work, and from that I'll go straight to the Y. By the time I come out of the Y, it will be time to go home to go to sleep to get up the next morning to start school all over again. And I'd try to find other things to do, yet I'd still make sure to find certain other things to keep me occupied just in case, when there's time, I don't go to the Y and things. So I'll just probably stay with my aunt and things and try to find good, popular friends, and when they do somethin' just think of laughing and say, "That's wrong and you know it." So you should leave and do something else or do another activity. (004)

Youth Centers

My ideas, I would say to join—go stay into sports. You know, if they would have a lot more like boys' clubs and after school centers, things like that, it keeps the kids off the streets, interest the kids to come in, I think there would be a lot less crime and kids in trouble.

So what you're saying, if there were more programs out there to keep the kids off the street and get them involved in something more productive, like playing sports or going to a youth center or something like that.

Yeah, something like that would be good. I talked to somebody about this, you know, it might sound funny, but my dream would be to open a gym for kids around my neighborhood where we got no boys' club and in the nearest park they sell drugs. I would like to open a gym where girls and boys, girls in one section on one floor, they just have like ballet and girls' things to do and downstairs have like basketball and softball teams, you know, something like that. I was planning it, you know, get the place, have somebody rich, you know, to invest money or donate money to that place. One person I had in mind was Donald Trump, you know. I always thought about writing him a letter and asking him for that little favor. A couple of other people, too, you know, like Tyson, you know, all the famous people with a lot of money that I think they won't mind, you know, donating money to that. (045)

SCHOOLS

Stricter Schools

That's good. What could anyone do to prevent delinquency so that you never had to have a place like this—kids never had to be sent away?

I think they could start having programs, and a lot of times that doesn't work, but try. And make the schools more stricter, like when you go in maybe get searched or something, and locker searches and things like that, and whatever they bring in there like alcohol or drugs, have that taken away. And maybe on the main road have more cops out there and things for the people who are out there—the high schoolers, teenagers who are out there will get caught, and hopefully that would get to their heads. (031)

Increased School Security

They should make sure that laws are enforced. There are stores all over the place that sell alcohol to minors. That has to stop. I used to sell drugs right in high school. It's common for the drug dealers to sell drugs right in high school; that has to stop. They need more undercover or security cops in school. (013)

School Uniforms

Can you think of any other ways that would help reduce crime in the streets?

In the schools, if all high schools and junior high schools had a uniform for kids to wear to school, everybody wear the same thing, that would be a lot better, too, 'cause nobody would know what anybody had if you wear a uniform.

That's interesting. So cut down on the peer pressure by everybody wearing the same thing—that's sort of what you went through in this program, isn't it?

Yep, that would help it a lot, though.

And what about jewelry and stuff like that in the schools?

If you wear jewelry—but there's jewelry, but like you said, you wear the same thing.

So cut everything out, same clothing for everybody.

Yes. (115)

Longer School Hours

And I'd make the school hours longer so that when they got out in the wintertime it would be dark.

What difference is that going to make?

They'll be tired.

By keeping their time occupied better?

That's right. (213)

School Curriculum

Learning How to Think

I would let my teachers know that I didn't understand something. I would let my teachers know that they shouldn't be telling me the answers. They should write them down for me. They should write the information down so I could understand it and I could get the answer myself, and not spoon-feed the kids out there because they're not learning nothing. They're just getting the answers from you. And you just pass them because you're giving them the answers. That's not keeping them into the knowledge that they need to go through school and to get what they need. If I was there I would go back and change my attitude and tell my teachers that I want to get my answers on my own, and I want to do my work by myself and understand it so I—when I go for a job and someone asks me what kind of math I can do, I can tell them I can do this or I can do that, that would be one of my major things. (020)

Classes on Delinquency

What do you think the schools can do to help prevent or help understand juvenile delinquent behavior?

There really isn't too much they can do, but they could have like a class, maybe. I'm not saying a regular class, but maybe a monthly session about the behavior of a juvenile delinquent so the students can understand, because some students don't really understand the problems that go on. (075)

Job Training

What kind of facilities do you think help kids?

Um, not lockup facilities, but facilities where they could require training, where they could help them out, tell them what's out there for them and what they can do with their lives. Open facilities, let you go places where you can learn, take you to places where people have jobs and show you what kind of jobs you can do. (038)

Psychological Skills Training

What would be a good way to prevent juvenile delinquency—what would be a good way to stop kids getting into trouble? What would be an effective way of preventing juvenile delinquency in America? What do you think needs to be done?

I still say to stop things like this, you need to know the skills that we been teached here. You know, I think it should be inside schools and stuff like that so that they can see that there is other things out there that they could do and other ways that they can get money besides standing on corners and hallways selling drugs and stuff like that, you know, running around robbing people. I think if the skills was being taught out in the public schools and stuff like that, I'm not saying that the kids won't be getting into trouble, but I'm saying they'll have a better chance of making the right decision before they get in trouble. I say they have a better chance of getting them a job. It doesn't matter how much money is being paid at that particular time because there's things in the [structured learning therapy], certain steps in there that they can learn and they'll realize that there is other ways that they can get money and stuff like that to prevent them going out there and getting themself in trouble. (057)

Self-Esteem Groups

Anything else, could the schools help?

I think the schools can help if they have like a special group about self-esteem and a group about peer pressure and things like that. A group to build up people positive so they can have better feelings about themselves, so they won't do them negative things. I think that would help a lot. (017)

MULTICOMPONENT INTERVENTIONS

Positive Models, Counseling

So let's talk about interventions and ways that juvenile delinquency can be reduced.

They can like start hanging around positive people, you know, in a good environment, positive environment, and they could also go for like counseling and stuff like that and get some help. I think it would help, you know, if they went for counseling. (081)

Parental Strictness, Youth Incarceration

The parents?

Um-hum.

Um, to spend more time with them. I think to be more strict with them 'cause I like when they were really strict and to the point. Sit down and do schoolwork with them, or go with them for an ice cream or something. Just share a special time or playing games at night, reading the Bible. That's what my family does. And sometimes sending them to a facility—that might work. 'Cause it did for me, that's what needed to be done. And there's a time when you just have to stop everything and say they do need to be put away. (016)

Counseling, Probation, Then Incarceration

What do you think should happen to kids who get into trouble?

I think the parents should talk to them and get them to go to counseling. If that don't work, they have to talk to a psychiatrist and probation. If that just doesn't work, just have them put away to learn their lesson. And just do it until they learn. (143)

Classes on Delinquency, Emergency Telephone Numbers, Halfway Houses

The best thing to do to stop juvenile delinquency would be to have structured delinquency classes set in regular city classrooms to learn about the problems of delinquency. Have regular normal classrooms with all the kids who have similar problems; a required class that the court makes them take. Before graduation you would have to take a test, role-play, etcetera, and eventually move back into a regular classroom setting. After graduation you should have follow-up and aftercare emergency numbers you can call if you are thinking of getting in trouble again. Additionally, halfway delinquent houses could be set up throughout the community. (163)

Scared Straight Programs, Parental Firmness, Parental Love

I'm not really sure if a Scared Straight program would do it, but it might. Little kids, I think everything scares them when they're

really young, and if you show them someone from when they
little not to do something, most likely they'll never do it when
they grow up. 'Cause they been taught that way, keep
encouraging them, keep reinforcing that until they grow up,
mature into adults. I think that it will help them a lot more and
they'll be a less percentage of people running away, going out
doing drugs, bad things out there. That will help a lot if you
keep reinforcing your rules in your house, in a strong and firm
way, but not too strong where the child could run away or leave
you or something like that. And always tell them that you love
them. If you really do love them, tell them that you love them.
Show them that you love them, not just say that you love them or
just show and not say it, 'cause they could assume that you're
saying it and not showing—then they might not care and they
might run away. (024)

Elimination of Drugs, Balanced School and Parental Discipline

*If you were going to fix this and if you were going to keep kids from
getting in trouble, what would you do? How would you keep kids from
getting in trouble, or what would you tell other people to do to keep
kids from getting in trouble?*

With the drugs I would try—I know I can't do this—but I would
try to get rid of every drug that there is, everything. Schools, I
would, some schools are real strict but some schools aren't strict
enough. I would get the schools that are real strict to calm down
a little bit on the kids and the ones that aren't strict to get a little
more stricter. That way the kids would be satisfied and the
teachers and principals would be satisfied with it and everything,
because back at my school, back where I live, it's not really any
fun and kids think, "Why go to school if there isn't any fun in
it?" If there were dances and stuff, more kids would be willing to
go and everything. With the family situation, I would try and
talk parents into letting kids have their freedom but not to the
full extent where they would get in trouble. Like set certain
rules, like in a group home, but not exactly like them, but like
the curfew, and give them certain chores they have to do. And
tell them rules they got to go by and stuff, like the phone—if
they want to use the phone, give them a limit. Don't try and take
the phone away from them because that will just make them mad,
and then they'll storm out of the house and go use somebody

else's phone. Try to talk to people before they get in a fight, to try to get them to take out their anger in another way. (095)

Safe Environment, Sports, Good Friends

If you were a mother and you had a boy, what would you do to keep him from becoming delinquent?

First, I would make sure I'm in an environment where it's not dangerous for him or me, make sure he's in school. I'd make sure he's in some kind of sport that keeps him busy and off the streets, make sure he's busy but at the same time that he's having fun with good friends.

What if you had a daughter?

I would do the same. I'd keep her near the house.

What if she wanted to get away from you?

I would sit her down and talk to her, and tell her, "You can have fun with people who do negative things, but you can have fun by going out to sports and school and with good kids, to the movies." And there's inappropriate ways to have fun, like smoking reefers and that. But if she's of age I would let her choose, but if she's young I would make decisions for her. (018)

Toys, Television, Parenting

In that last statement you talked about some things that may have prevented delinquency. Would you like to talk about them a little more?

Yes, well, what I think is that if a person have a child at an early age, and they didn't want it or wanted it, but if they gonna have it, bring them up in the right way, not in the wrong way. Teach them right from wrong. Try to put them with kids you see that are positive. Like I notice that most little boys and girls—little boys mostly they get guns for Christmas or guns for their birthday, but looking at TV showing negative stuff, they might think, "Well, when I get older I can use one of these." Like buy them education things, like buy them things that teaches them about drugs and about people relationships, schoolwork. Because if you don't teach them that, they're going to turn into a negative person. In order to have positive things, you got to teach them more positive than negative. When you discipline them, discipline them the right way. Like don't abuse them, like don't hit them so hard they bleed or something. Abuse them the right way, like tell them, "You can't go out and play" or some other kind of punishment. Like do some homework but in a different way. If you take that situation and start hitting them, they're going to be mad at you and they're going to do what they want to do, and that's gonna cause a big problem. But if you just give them homework and they sit down and maybe they'll understand and say, "Well, the reason I got to do this is because I went outside and I swore." (002)

Hotlines, Probation, Drug Education, Teen Centers

Can you think of anything anyone can do to solve the delinquency problem?

There's programs out in the community that kids can go to, if they make them more where kids can really reach out and touch them. Like they have programs where you have to wait a couple of days to get involved in them—better to have like a hotline, instant help. And I think that probation is good for kids who have a lot of problems. I think that if probation officers spent a lot of time with the kids, you know, it seems like they just go and see them every week, and they don't do too much to help them. If they'd explore into their week, and ask how their week was and what problems they had and give them solutions. I think a lot of drugs cause more delinquency. If they could prevent kids from taking a lot of drugs—but I know that's impossible. In schools, if they had help in schools and talked about drugs and if they give them something real positive to look forward to. Like positive groups and maybe a teenage place where all teenagers can go instead of in the streets and wanting to do bad things. (038)

Early Parenting, Values Training, Tougher Drug Laws

Well, the parents can bring their children up the right way. If their children want something, not to automatically give it to them or not to start giving it to them and when you start to pull it away they still want it, and they gonna find some way to get it. You have to have—you have to condition them, to let them know, you have to start when they're young, when they're starting to learn how to talk, you have to show them values. You have to teach them good values because my mom always told me if you have a tree and it's starting to grow and it leans over and you let it grow, it's gonna stay leaned over, but if you take a stick and fix it and let it grow straight, it will help. So that's how I see it—you

have to get them while they're young. When they're too old, it's
hard, they don't want to listen to that. I think schools—I think
children should start learning things when they starting in
kindergarten. They should learn sex ed, and they should always
learn things about their values. 'Cause some kids they don't
know, 'cause when they ask their parents, "What's that? What is
that they're doing?" they try to cover it up and make it look nice,
and the child doesn't know, so when they grow up they try to
find out what it is. I think the government should enforce a law
that the schools should teach values, and they should teach sex
ed, too, and make stricter rules on kids selling drugs, 'cause I
know young people, they say, "Well, I sell it 'cause I know I'm
not going to jail—I'm too young to go to jail." I think they
should enforce more laws to the younger people who are selling
drugs. Now the older people, when they want to sell their drugs
they get someone young. Real little ones, 'cause they can't do
time. They'll come right back out. (036)

MISCELLANEOUS

Nothing Works

I really feel that nothing truly works with kids. Nothing society
or family can do really matters because the kids are going to
experiment and will have to learn and find out for themselves.
People in my community, friends, family, the police, lawyers, even
the judges warned me, but I did it anyway. (139)

*What do you think would be an effective way of preventing juvenile
delinquency?*

There won't be no way because it'll never stop. There won't be
no way. I have no idea to that question, no idea. To me it's like
they coming in and out, most of them will be dead or back to
jail, so I can't answer that question. (213)

Peers Helping Peers

Well, sometimes kids can also help other kids, and sometimes
adults can help kids. I think since people get delinquent from
their peer pressures, maybe if those delinquent friends turned
right that they would maybe follow. I think that peers can help
peers. (034)

Prosocial Models

If you decided to become a mother and you were still living [in your community], what kinds of things would you do to make sure your child doesn't have problems?

Well, one thing if I was becoming a mother, my family, my aunt right away would help me out. I would try, like I would ask my aunt some advices and things and to show me how to raise my child 'cause she had experience. She had a child at a young early age now, and her child does not disrespect her or curse in the house. He does not disrespect her. So since I see that, I would ask my aunt for some advices about how she grew him up by herself, just in case if I don't have my mate with me to help me raise that child, and she would give me some advice and I would try to take it and help myself and my baby. (004)

Pictures of the Future

What would you do?

Maybe like showing them future pictures or something and saying, "This is how your life will be." (008)

Movies of Drug Effects

Or what they say, like put on plays, show a demonstration, like get movies about drugs and what they do to you and like when you stop, what you go through, what happens to you the rest of your life. You might be, like, dumb. You might not get a job—you might be poor. You might be an old man that somebody's gonna throw you a dime and you can't buy no food with that, be a garbage picker and all that. And people, I don't think they want to do that. If they really looked and saw these things, they would think twice, because when I watch the news—I never really did harmful stuff—but when I watch the news I can picture myself and say, "No, I don't want nobody shooting me or me shooting nobody else. There are people who'll get back at you even though you don't think they saw you, but they will get back at you." (002)

Earlier Work Permits

You say work. Working at a younger age?

Like kids who are 12. That is where a lot of it starts. Maybe even
9 years old. Getting those kids interested in job careers. It seems
a little young, but sometimes you run out of time and things like
that. You get them involved with different jobs while they are
younger, and then when they are 16 and old enough to get a real
job, they'll have more background on what type of job they want.
Maybe a job in a hospital, a job cleaning out horse stalls out in
the country. (200)

Counseling Advertisements

*You've lived near a lot of big cities and led a street kind of life. If you
were a counselor, how would you reach the kids?*

I'd advertise on TV or a number to call whenever you need to
and put up brochures in laundromats. Places where some
runaways might hang out. I would go around myself and put
brochures around and posters and stuff with numbers. Mostly
like advertisements and publications, 'cause the only other way to
do it.

*You say a phone number—something easy to remember. Do you think it
should be staffed 24 hours a day?*

Yes, something with an operator 24 hours a day. (230)

Closing of Housing Projects

*Do you have any other ideas about some ways that would prevent a lot
of the juvenile delinquency that's going on, that's taking place out
there now?*

Close down a lot of projects because that's where they're coming
from—a lot of trouble at the projects, make regular houses
instead of projects because that's where a lot of trouble is coming
from nowadays. (135)

Videos of Incarcerated Youths

I was thinkin' maybe we should have like a video camera. Like
videotape every girl that comes in here, and then maybe have a
videotape of all the girls at [the state delinquency facility] so we
can show the other people in the community what it's like to be
in a facility like this or maybe even try it.

That might scare them?

Right, like scare them. (023)

Celebrity Campaigns

If really important people became involved in campaigning to stop delinquency, it would drop. Rock stars and political figures could spread the message "Stop crime, crime is wrong, drugs are wrong." Society should boost up this message. (023)

More Police

If there was a city that had a delinquency problem, what could the city do to stop it?

Organize some programs to help kids, and to stop drug dealers they should have cops on every corner all night long to stop it. (034)

More Trusting Police

If kids are hanging out, the police should approach them with care and concern, rather than with that authoritative stare and intimidation. . . . The police should get to know the kids, so the kids will learn to trust them and turn to them if they are in trouble. (049)

Less Indifferent Police

The police departments could do a hell of a lot more than they're doing now. Right now, you can see a police car drive by and you can be sitting right there doing a crime, doing crack or something, and a cop will go right past you and look over and smile at you and just keep going. We should have better police coverage to do a better job. (138)

Less Biased Police

And for people to have a little more trust in Black people, you know. Cops see a Black person walking and say, "Oh, God, you're about to steal." You know it's not like that in all cases. And a White person will walk in and they'll turn their eyes away. I don't like to go in stores no more 'cause every time I walk in a store they look at me, like no big stores like _____. (037)

Money

So what are some things you could think of, ways to prevent it or reduce it—is there anything that you could tell me to reduce juvenile delinquency as it is? What can we do?

If there was ways for juveniles to get money legally, at least a nice sum of money, there wouldn't be that much crime. (115)

If every kid from 8 to 16 years old got a 5-dollar allowance, maybe that would keep them from stealing if they had some money and knew they would get an allowance every week. They need to have more jobs for kids, things like delivering newspapers or groceries or washing cars. If kids could get money from jobs, it could keep them busy and keep money in their pocket so they wouldn't have the urge to steal. (099)

Is there anything that you can think that your parents could do to keep you from getting into more trouble?

Sure they could, but I just don't know how I'd put it. Most of the times they have to give you everything you want. I don't know, maybe an allowance. Sometimes if you have money it keeps you out of trouble, not always, but most of the time.

How would the money keep you out of trouble?

You just got it in your pocket, and you feel happy about it.

So you'd be happier if you had money to spend?

Right, like I kind of stole money to buy a stereo.

Stole money from who?

From the videogames. Then I stole the engine just to have it. My parents wouldn't buy one. I used to have this go-cart that I bought myself, 'cause I used to have a paper route a long time ago, and I bought this go-cart with the money I saved up and that was like my fun. Then it broke, so I didn't have it anymore. So I kind of got into stealing, and so I finally stole another engine and I got caught for it. Then my stereo broke in my car, so when these guys were stealing the money, I joined them. And then I saved up the money to buy a stereo. (103)

So parents could give kids more money to spend, and then they wouldn't have to steal.

Hotlines

What I feel? Well, they do have family court that a lot of us go through. It could help them, but I think what they should do is . . . you know, alcohol problems, like you think you're becoming a drug addict or alcoholic, they have numbers to call. I think they should set something up like that in the community. Then, if they really feel that they are going to do something wrong or commit a crime or do something really bad, they should call and, you know, talk it out with them. So that maybe they can avoid, you know, getting in trouble in the community. Especially if they are recently released from a facility and they haven't done anything, and then all of a sudden their friends are starting to do it, talk it out with somebody, have counselors.

OK, so hotline type things?

Yes. (060)

Antishoplifting Sensors

I think they should get those little sensors, you know, on the doors if someone walks out with something. That would stop a lot of it, like cameras everywhere, I mean that would stop a lot of it because if you just see a camera you won't do it—I wouldn't.

So you think it should be more obvious that they're watching people in a store?

Yeah, because when you walk in there, you know, most managers are stupid. They're going to be looking for somebody who's looking over their shoulder. Like I said, if you just walk out real calm, like 1 out of every 100 times you'll get caught. That's what my friend told me, and it was about my 100th time I got caught. So that's my theory. (101)

Delinquents as Store Detectives

No idea is a dumb idea.

I think the store managers should hire people like me, that know how to look for shoplifters, because everybody thinks a shoplifter is going to be looking over their shoulder, and after you do it for a while you don't even look, you just do it. Like they have these little short, fat managers that just look for the nervous people, you know. They don't look for people who go right to the checkout counter. As far as the cops, I don't think there's really nothing they can do. And probation, I don't know much about probation other than I've been on probation for about 3 weeks. (101)

Vans to Pick Up Truants

They used to have this policy where these vans would go around picking up the kids who were skipping school. This seemed to help. Most parents don't even know their kids are skipping school. Some parents bring their kids to school and make sure they go in the building. (018)

Alcohol-Free Bars and Dances

What do you think would be an effective way of preventing juvenile delinquency? If you were put in charge of a program out in the world to prevent juvenile delinquency, to prevent kids from getting into trouble, what would you do?

I'd do what they're starting to do now, is to set up teenage nonalcoholic bars and dance floors and stuff. But I'd have them a lot stricter, like the kids get searched and stuff, 'cause now they got these things, they bring all the drugs and alcohol inside instead of out in the streets. That's a little bit better, but it's still there. (047)

Psychologists at Arcades

What would you do as far as the arcades and stuff? Would you have counselors available for the kids to talk to?

Yeah, because no matter where you go, somebody's going to end up arguing or fighting. So I guess in the arcade I would have a manager working there, and I would probably have a psychologist there. And if a kid starts fighting just bring him in, the first time talk to them, the second time just kick him out. First of all, explain to him that fighting isn't the way to live and have the two kids talk and whatever, same thing for the Y—I'd have a counselor there, too. (097)

Individualized Interventions

What can actually be done to reduce kids' getting in trouble or prevent them from getting into trouble?

Well, you should ask them first. Ask them, like spend time talking to them. Ask them, "What will make you stop doing this?" and they'll tell you. As long as it ain't nothing terrible, they will tell you what will really make them stop. Then you just follow along with them. Like, for instance, I was in a lot of trouble and everything, and when they really got down to me, I really just wanted to live with my father. That's where I'm at now, living with my father, and they talked to me and stuff, and I finally got a chance to live with my father, and everything came out fine. (166)

Rewarding Nondelinquency

One thing I thought about is like give some kind of privileges.

This is the way you think the system could be improved to help kids to keep them from getting into trouble?

Like school, they should give, like, every month or maybe every semester some kind of thing for people that haven't skipped or missed much school.

Privileges—like what do you mean?

Like maybe an hour lunch or a free day, something—I don't know—something that you'd want, that most kids would want, something to work for, you know, if you didn't take that skip day. Maybe the same for the community. Kids that aren't really in trouble, maybe it would be hard in some communities because some communities are really big, but base some kind of—I don't know—maybe like a carnival or something where, like, kids that weren't in trouble or anything or have kept themselves out of trouble or have gotten into trouble and have done everything they possibly could to keep out of trouble—some kind of privileges like that. I don't know exactly, it would be kind of hard, but like a carnival or a fair.

Something for the kids to work at or go to or what?

Something they could work for besides "Yeah, you're a good kid" and all that. Something where if they worked for it, it would be worth it, like they'd get paid back somehow for their being so good all the time, you know, like no speeding tickets, you know, maybe help with insurance or something, you know, like maybe the community could pay like 30 percent or something like that, you know, just a little bit on the insurance. I don't know—some kind of privileges that kids would want to work for and stay out of trouble and feel that they've earned something. (105)

CHAPTER 6

Comparisons and Implications

In the present chapter, we seek to examine and compare the causation and intervention thinking of our two types of experts—by training and by experience. We also attempt to draw implications from these perspectives and their comparison for both heightened etiological clarity and enhanced intervention potency.

CAUSATION

Both the professionals and our youth sample are primarily social learning theorists, though the professionals are also much more. As Table 4 recapitulates, the professionals offer a broad range of theoretical positions—micro to macro; simple to complex; intrapersonal, interpersonal, and societal. As noted and concretized in chapter 2, professional etiological thinking has moved from early constitutional notions and tautological psychoanalytic speculation, to sound but too unidimensional sociological perspectives, to more sophisticated and data-based biogenetic and psychological theorizing. These efforts have most recently been followed by multicomponent etiological positions that conjointly emphasize physiological, psychological, and sociological or sociopolitical causative factors. These multicomponent theories—most of which have a distinct social learning emphasis—are clearly consistent with the general trend toward multicausal thinking that has emerged in many domains of personality theory and psychopathology theory in recent years. Stated otherwise, much current professional theorizing about the roots of juvenile delinquency points to the concurrent influence of a physiological predisposition; certain specific personality qualities; and an environment (family, peers, school, neighborhood) whose modeling displays, harshness, financial poverty, labeling propensities, and other qualities serve a delinquency-promoting role.

TABLE 4   Professional Perspectives on Causation

CONSTITUTIONAL THEORIES

Anthropometrics
Endocrine disorders
Somatotyping

PSYCHOLOGICAL THEORIES

Psychoanalytic theory
Personality trait theory
        Extroversion, neuroticism, psychoticism
        Psychopathy
        Moral reasoning
        Conceptual level
        Irresponsible thinking
        Rational choicefulness
Social learning theory

SOCIOLOGICAL THEORIES

Strain theory
        Anomie
        Reactance
        Differential opportunity
Subcultural theory
        Differential association
        Generating milieu
        Differential identification
        Cultural conflict
        Illicit means
        Situational determinism
Control theory
        Social bonding
        Drift-neutralization
        Containment
Labeling theory
Radical theory

BIOGENETIC AND NEUROHORMONAL THEORIES

Genetic transmission
Arousal theory
Seizuring theory
Hemispheric functioning
Androgen exposure

MULTICOMPONENT THEORIES

Differential opportunity theory
Social learning theory
Differential association–differential reinforcement theory
Social developmental theory
Integrated learning theory
Other multicomponent theories
   Criminal opportunity
   Social disorganization
   Control, strain, and labeling
   Genetic predisposition and social learning
   Control, strain, and social learning
   Socioanalytic
   Interpersonal maturity

The youths, as reflected in Table 5, are primarily social learning theorists. They speak mainly from experience. They share what has happened to them or to others they know and only rarely convey what they might imagine. They point to lived events and themes, not genes, sociological forces, or other unobservable constructs. In both their monocausal and multicomponent viewpoints, they singly or in combination point to the etiological influence of dysfunctional families, peers, and drugs. Although a wide and often novel array of other perceived causes are also identified by individual youths, it is clearly this family, peer, and drug constellation that prevails. The externalizing character of these identified causes is, in effect, heightened as it contrasts with the almost total absence of perceived causes internal to the youths. None spoke of one or another personality dimension or flaw, and but one youth made explicit an "I am responsible" theme. The world, in the youths' view, acts upon them in hostile, punitive, compelling, attractive, consciousness-clouding, or other ways, and delinquent behavior is the response. In a simplistic sense, it is as if they perceived the world of delinquency causation in stimulus-response rather than stimulus-organism-response terms.

TABLE 5 Youth Perspectives on Causation

FAMILY DYSFUNCTION

General influence
Harsh parental discipline
Lax parental discipline
Inconsistent discipline
Parental rejection
Parental oversolicitousness
Parental disharmony
Family violence
Single parenting
Family disconnectedness
Parental models
Sibling models

PEERS

equal person
<u>Peer</u> pressure *-plans*
Peer acceptance
Peer modeling

DRUGS

Drug-taking effects
Money-seeking effects

POVERTY

SCHOOL

LABELING

MULTICOMPONENT PERSPECTIVES

Peers, drugs, parents, inhibition
Peers, drugs, parents, absence of support
Peers, drugs, parents, school
Peers, drugs, parents, school, abuse
Peers, drugs, parents, school, poverty, neighborhood norms

MISCELLANEOUS

Intrapersonal
>   Bad genes
>   Fun
>   Thrill
>   Boredom
>   Power
>   Notoriety
>   Oppositional Feelings

Familial
>   Providing financial help
>   Intergenerational transmission
>   Racism
>   Expressive act
>   Teen fatherhood
>   Failure to be physically punished

Environmental
>   Seeking respect
>   Older youth influence
>   Police abuse
>   Movies
>   Television
>   Music
>   City living
>   Getting off drugs
>   Being good at being bad

INTERVENTION

Approximately two thirds of all adjudicated juvenile delinquents will recidivate, most within 6 months of release from incarceration (Maltz, 1984; Rutter & Giller, 1983). On the basis of this and related bottom-line criteria, it is clear that available delinquency interventions are still of modest efficacy. As such, it is vital that a broad and varied range of approaches, differing in target level and procedural content, be created, implemented, and evaluated. It is precisely this state of affairs that we discussed in chapter 4 and have summarized in

Table 6. A wide variety of both youth-directed and system-directed approaches exist. They combine to present what we view as a healthy, experimental, creative array—multimodal, multilevel, multitargeted. Older approaches (e.g., individual and group psychotherapy) have appropriately begun to decrease in frequency of use as outcome evidence has revealed their lack of impact. Conversely, newer approaches (e.g., various cognitive and skill-development behavioral procedures) have become more ascendant in response to encouraging efficacy evaluations. Yet other approaches, especially probation and parole, continue to be most used quite independently of serious evaluations of effectiveness, whereas still other strategies, highly promising in concept, have yet to be sufficiently implemented and evaluated (e.g., the more macro-level, system-directed interventions). In general, the intervention efforts of such disciplines as psychology, criminology, sociology, and other professional areas reveal an active, diverse, creative, and, in some of their procedures, promising array of prevention and remediation techniques and perspectives. Success to date has been modest, but an appropriate effort appears to be well underway.

Our sample of delinquent youths shared a totally, even dramatically, different set of perspectives on delinquency intervention. Though certainly not lacking in either creativity or novelty, their central theme by far was punishment. Perhaps standing in testament to the notion that harshness breeds harshness, that many abused persons "pass it on" and are themselves abusive, punishment themes predominated in our 250 interviews. Table 7 summarizes these data. Although a number of interesting and seemingly implementable recreational and miscellaneous offerings should be noted as exceptions, the youths' proposed parenting, school, and especially criminal justice system interventions are largely repeated calls for harshness, strictness, punitiveness, control, and, in a few cases, even brutality. Incarceration, they collectively urge, should be mandatory, longer, harsher, and devoid of mitigating pleasures. Parenting and schooling should be stricter, stricter earlier, and more readily punitive.

But let us not overstate. Though the shadow of punitive themes tends to cloud and push aside the more positive youth suggestions, a number of the latter did emerge. Several youths urged greater use of parent training and enhanced parent-youth communication. Schools, they held, ought not only to be made stricter, but might also utilize a number of seemingly valuable and relevant curricular innovations. And several of these miscellaneous proposals seem novel, doable, and pregnant with potential.

TABLE 6   Professional Perspectives on Intervention

YOUTH-DIRECTED INTERVENTIONS

Judicial and administrative approaches
        Diversion
        Probation
        Parole
Setting-based approaches
        Institutional interventions
        Community-based interventions
Therapeutic approaches
        Individual psychotherapy
        Group psychotherapy
        Prescriptive programming
        Behavior modification
                Contingency management approaches
                Cognitive approaches
Other youth-directed approaches
        Educational
        Vocational
        Therapeutic camping and wilderness programs
        Positive peer culture
        Guided group intervention
        Reality therapy
        Restitution programs
        Pharmacotherapy
        Shock incarceration or boot camps
        Scared Straight programs

SYSTEM-DIRECTED INTERVENTIONS

Peer-oriented approaches
Community-oriented approaches
Family-oriented approaches
        Psychodynamic
        Family systems
        Contingency management
        Skills training
School-oriented approaches

TABLE 7 Youth Perspectives on Intervention

PUNISHMENT

Incarceration alternatives
        Incarceration
        Harsher incarceration
        Mandatory incarceration
        Sentencing of youths as adults
        Longer incarceration
        Life sentences
        Life sentences without food
        Incarceration of parents
        Incarceration with attack dog
Other punishments
        Stricter parents and schools
        Involuntary drug rehabilitation
        Scared Straight programs, other demonstrations
        Curfew
        More gun use
        House arrest by parents

PARENTING

Parent training
Parent-youth communication
Other parenting-associated interventions
        Stricter parenting
        Early discipline
        Early adoption for unwanted children
        Parental love
        Values training

COUNSELING

Nonspecific suggestions
Family counseling
Peer counseling
Intensified probation counseling
Aggression Replacement Training

RECREATION

Videogames, sports
Parks, concerts, arcades
Hobbies, drama
Gymnastics
Recreation centers
Neighborhood clubs
Arcades
YMCAs
Youth centers

SCHOOLS

Stricter schools
Increased school security
School uniforms
Longer school hours
School curriculum
       Learning how to think
       Classes on delinquency
       Job training
       Psychological skills training
       Self-esteem groups

MULTICOMPONENT INTERVENTIONS

Positive models, counseling
Parental strictness, youth incarceration
Counseling, probation, then incarceration
Classes on delinquency, emergency telephone numbers,
    halfway houses
Scared Straight programs, parental firmness, parental love
Elimination of drugs, balanced school and parental discipline
Safe environment, sports, good friends
Toys, television, parenting
Hotlines, probation, drug education, teen centers
Early parenting, values training, tougher drug laws

MISCELLANEOUS

Nothing works
Peers helping peers
Prosocial models

TABLE 7   *(cont'd)*

MISCELLANEOUS   (cont'd)

Pictures of the future
Movies of drug effects
Earlier work permits
Counseling advertisements
Closing of housing projects
Videos of incarcerated youths
Celebrity campaigns
More police
More trusting police
Less indifferent police
Less biased police
Money
Hotlines
Antishoplifting sensors
Delinquents as store detectives
Vans to pick up truants
Alcohol-free bars and dances
Psychologists at arcades
Individualized interventions
Rewarding nondelinquency

IMPLICATIONS FOR PREVENTION AND REMEDIATION

The present project has had two broad purposes. Its first and perhaps primary goal has been largely reportorial—to obtain and share the etiology- and intervention-relevant phenomenology of a broad sample of delinquent youths. In examining this phenomenology and comparing it to that reflected in the professional literature, we seek to obtain heuristic leads to understand juvenile delinquency better and, especially, to prevent and reduce its occurrence. In these latter regards, we first reject our youths' repeated call for greater punitiveness. Although the relevant evidence is not all one-sided, the predominant outcomes of punishment evaluations are negative (Axelrod & Apache, 1982; Bandura, 1973; Goldstein & Keller, 1987). In part because punishment fails to teach new, alternative responses and in part because its effectiveness has been shown to be a complex function of its likelihood, consistency, immediacy, duration, severity, alternatives, and more, the behavior change consequences of punishment (e.g., reprimands, corporal punishment) seem very often to be but a temporary alteration in behavior at best.

There also appears to be a second negative implication for intervention in our youths' commentaries. We refer to their major propensity for externalization. So many of the interventions traditionally offered to delinquent youths and traditionally largely ineffective in changing their behavior—individual and group psychotherapy, reality therapy, and Scared Straight Programs—rely heavily on an internal locus of etiology. Youths need in these approaches to see *themselves* as largely responsible for the causes of their behavior and for its modification. These are laudable amenability goals, but not prescriptively available for those interventions that heavily depend on them.

What should we be affirmatively responsive to among our sample's perspectives? Youths have told us in dozens of ways, as has the developmental literature on adolescence, that they are immensely responsive to peer influence. It is not a great conceptual or procedural leap to urge that this perspective be responded to and that new and creative ways be devised and implemented for "capturing" or co-opting such peer influence in constructive, prosocial, nondelinquent directions. Suggestions for peers helping peers, peer counseling, or "getting down with the positive group" are promising leads. Our own research group (Goldstein & Glick, 1987) has begun forming The Angerbusters, a "prosocial gang" of recently deincarcerated delinquent youths. Guided group interaction and positive peer culture techniques used not in isolation, but as part of multicomponent intervention programming, may prove to be valuable directions. Other such peer-driven alternatives exist, and many more may well be worth constructing.

A number of other youth-originated proposals seem deserving of serious consideration. Certainly one such notion is the increased utilization of parent training. Mercer and Renda's (1985) Taking Care Program, designed for incarcerated delinquents who are fathers, is one such effort already showing promising (if impressionistic) outcomes. Other youth suggestions we feel may prove worthwhile include rewarding nondelinquent behavior, use of school uniforms, a delinquency hotline, safe house respites, alcohol-free bars and dances, and, in a contemporary concretization of the decades-old spirit of detached-worker gang programs, the use of psychologists at arcades. In these and still other intervention regards, the youths have spoken. We indeed ought to listen.

We have two final observations. The first is that, taken as a collective, the diverse professional and youth perspectives on causation converge on the broad conclusion that juvenile delinquency is a complexly determined behavior having multiple causality. Complex behaviors require complex, multifaceted interventions for their alteration. We have elaborated this perspective elsewhere (Goldstein & Glick, 1987; Goldstein et al., 1989), and we simply wish to emphasize here the data-based belief that a multilevel (e.g., youth-directed *and* system-directed), multimodal (e.g., cognitive, affective, behavioral) intervention program is an especially potent strategy for altering that difficult-to-change complex of behaviors called juvenile delinquency.

Second, our ability to understand the roots of juvenile delinquency and effect its prevention and reduction will also be advanced, we believe, if we more fully remember and respond to the fact that delinquents are also adolescents. In fact, with no implication intended that this developmental stance mitigates the seriousness of adolescent crime, or that we are assuming a "boys will be boys" attitude, it ought to be said that delinquents often are *hyperadolescents,* and this status must, in ways yet to be determined, be factored into our causal thinking and intervention selection. Why do we venture to call such youths hyperadolescents? In the phenomenological spirit of this book, let us have the youths illustratively speak for themselves, reflecting the following quintessential adolescent qualities.

Striving for a Unique Identity

I don't think really anybody is happy with their life—everybody has to go through changes to figure out what they really are. One day a kid could be the sweetest little kid on earth, the next day they're wearing all black, they got big earrings in their ears, they got eyeliner going all the way around their head, the left side of their head is all shaved off, they dyed their hair four different colors, and they're wearing these clothes that look like they came out of Salvation Army. I used to wear the strangest clothes—white ruffle socks with pink sneakers and army green pantyhose, a white skirt with four different shirts, and my makeup and hair, I had all kinds of makeup with all colors of lipstick with sparkles in it. (093)

Oppositional Feelings

So a lot of it you think is family then?

Whether it's your parents or not, if somebody tells you to do something and you don't want to do it, you're going to do the opposite. Like if somebody tells you you gotta go to school, you're not going to go, or if somebody says you gotta stay home, they're gonna leave. (095)

What causes kids to get in trouble?

It could be boredom, or if you just want to do it to get to somebody, like to get to your parents or get their attention or to get your parents angry at you and do the opposite of what they say. A number of things. (099)

Hyperindependence

Because, like, the people that love me, they wanted to control me, but I didn't want nobody to control me. I wanted to do what I wanted to do, and I wanted to have fun, and I had fun in a negative way. (021)

That's why I didn't want to go to school—because people were telling me I had to go to school and I said, "No, I don't, do you want to watch me?" 'cause I didn't like people telling me what to do. I still hate it when people tell me what to do.

Do you feel that got you in trouble?

What can I say? I'm stubborn and rebellious at the same time and the two don't mix . . . people pushing you, saying you gotta do this, you gotta do that. If people push you, say the hell with them, you know. I just want to say to them, why don't you stick your finger up your ass and rotate, so I'm serious 'cause nobody in this world has their life straight enough to tell other people how to live theirs. (093)

Asking for Limits

You wanted to live with your father after that?

Yeah, and I just started leaving the house when I wanted to, and I started doing what I felt like, and at the time my mother was pregnant, so she didn't know how to stop me from doing all this stuff. She tried to talk to me, but what I really needed was somebody that could control me. I know I could control myself, but somebody who could tell me what to do and don't get in any trouble and I could listen to them. I mean somebody that's like strict. I really wanted to live with my dad, and I really wanted to behave and not do any shoplifting and stuff. So I decided to let the counselors talk to me, and I really wanted to live with my dad, and I'm very happy where I'm staying now. (033)

Externalization of Responsibility

The causes are that people shouldn't leave buildings unlocked. Like the building we went into, there was a big huge hole in the side of the log so we just jumped up and walked in. So the causes are that people just don't care, and they leave their buildings— they don't board up holes they have or anything. They know kids are gonna get in there, and they leave beer right up in the windows so kids can see it. (061)

Peer Pressure, Exploration, Rebelliousness

Why do kids begin with alcohol? Why do they take up alcohol, or why do they take up drugs for the first time?

I think it would be to be down with the crowd or just to try it to see what it's like, to see if they like it or because their parents told them not to do it. Some people will do it just to rebel against their parents. (047)

Difficulty Being Independent

That they think that once they hit like 13, 14, gettin' into their teens, they can handle their own problems on their own. They think that I'm independent now 'cause I'm a teenager. I'm going into the adolescence. I think I should handle my own problems. But that's not always true because it's not easy to be independent by yourself. You need people back there supporting you, helping you. I say a lot of the teenagers now are guys who get into trouble and be delinquent and all that because they don't have enough support from their parents or from other people. 'Cause the other people just let them do what they want to do, and they just get into more trouble until someone has to make the decision for them. (020)

We view this book as a beginning step on a phenomenological path we hope others will follow. Our experts-by-experience have indeed had much of value to say, both implicitly and explicitly. Juvenile delinquency is a phenomenon that is difficult to understand and difficult to change. Youths' real-life expertise has still much more to offer. We hope others will seek it and truly listen when these youngsters speak.

Project Description and Interviewer Instructions

PROJECT DESCRIPTION

Although psychology, social work, education, and other professional fields have made important contributions to our understanding of the roots of juvenile delinquency and our means for intervening to reduce its frequency and severity, delinquency continues in the United States at high levels, and recidivism rates indicate that our efforts at prevention and intervention are at best only partially effective. Are there, this project asks, other types of experts to turn to for useful impressions, opinions, and speculations? We believe there are, that such other expertise has rarely been used and is worth pursuing. We refer not to yet another professional expert group but, instead, to experts-by-experience, juvenile delinquents themselves.

We therefore are seeking the views of delinquent youths regarding the *causes* of juvenile delinquency and the means for its *prevention and reduction*. We hope to obtain a number of tape-recorded interviews, conducted by staff familiar with the youths who participate and focused on gathering the opinions and experiences of these youths. We wish to keep our interview procedure open ended, so we have not developed a set list of interview questions. Instead, we more simply want staff who relate well to the particular youths to open the two topics that are the focus of this project—(a) the *causes* of juvenile delinquency and (b) interventions to *prevent* or *reduce* it—and then to follow the youths' responses in order to elicit their full thinking on these issues. Thus, any single interview might last only 15 minutes, or it might take an hour or more.

Please have the interviewer carefully *check and test* the tape recorder and verify that it is recording just before each interview.

We are going to get the interviews typed, and we must have good recordings. In our pilot work on this project, we conducted both individual and group (3 to 5 youths) interviews, and both alternatives are fine for this request (if group, be especially sure the recorder is picking up *all* members). Interviewees can be male or female delinquent youths in facility, group home, aftercare, or other settings.

I really appreciate your willingness to help out on this project. For further procedural information, all project interviewers should read the interviewer instruction sheet, along with this project description. If you wish any further details, or if there are questions, I'm at [telephone number].

Arnold P. Goldstein, PhD
Syracuse University

INTERVIEWER INSTRUCTIONS

Interview style and content should strive to blend relevance to the proposed project's information-obtaining goals with the interview "looseness" and flexibility necessary to obtain rich and individualized interviewee responses. We agree with Bogdan and Biklen's (1982) description of this strategy:

> In keeping with the qualitative tradition of attempting to capture the subject's own words, and letting the analysis emerge, interview schedules . . . generally allow for open-ended responses and are flexible enough for the observer to note and collect data on unexpected dimensions of the topic. (p. 71)

Yet interviews cannot be too unstructured or unfocused, or relevant data will fail to be obtained. Thus, the general sense of our planned interview(s) for each participant youth may best be described as commencing in a topic-relevant but essentially nondirective, open-ended, and broadly structured manner, and moving progressively, *only if necessary when not enough response is offered by the youth,* to a more specific, closed-ended, and narrowly structured interviewer style. Open-ended questions such as, Why do you think kids get in trouble? or, What's your opinion about why juvenile delinquency happens? or, What do you think can be done so that there would be less juvenile delinquency in America? *may* have to be followed by more direct questions of intermediate structure—for example, Do you think a guy's family or how he's brought up has anything to do with getting into crime? or, What about someone's friends? Does that have anything to do with getting into trouble?—then, if appropriate, by such highly specific questions as, If someone's friends go straight or get in trouble, how does that affect a guy's own behavior? or, What if a father beats a kid a lot—what's the effect on the kid and whether he gets in trouble? How much questioning will be necessary, and how direct or specific the questions must be, will be up to each interviewer and his or her judgment about how each interview is going.

We will not intentionally turn our planned interviews into journeys through youths' personal histories—that is, we will not plan to inquire into the reasons they believe they committed delinquent acts, or how such behavior could have been prevented, or their personal or familial histories. However, our pilot interviews and more general experiences with delinquent youths strongly suggest that much of what participating youths will have to say will at times be of this personalized nature, revealing richly detailed events, experiences, and perceptions of both an historical and contemporary nature of considerable relevance to project goals. We will welcome such information. We will not press for it and will respect each youth's right to keep the responses more or less depersonalized and about "the other guy." But when personal accounts are entered into, questions should gently, nonprobingly follow the informational leads thus provided.

Interview participation by the youths should be voluntary, anonymous, and as pleasant, interesting, and noncoercive as possible. Interviewers should seek to have participating youths experience their project roles as *research partners,* rather than as deviant objects of outside scrutiny. To concretize this spirit, in addition to using the types of open-ended questions and gentle questioning styles described here, interviewers should carefully explain the project's intentions, assure anonymity, and pay continuing attention to building and maintaining an interviewer-interviewee relationship characterized by respect and trust.

To encourage both depth and breadth of response, interviewers can employ a variety of interview sequences. Some youths can be interviewed once, whereas others who may have a great deal to say can participate in two or more individual interviews. Some interviewing, confidentiality considerations permitting, may be done in small groups. Any questions about the interview or the project as a whole will gladly be answered. Please call me at [telephone number].

Thank you for your assistance. Your participation in this project is very much appreciated.

Arnold P. Goldstein, PhD
Syracuse University

References

Abadinsky, H. (1979). *Social service in criminal justice.* Englewood Cliffs, NJ: Prentice-Hall.

Abbott, J. H. (1981). *In the belly of the beast.* New York: Random House.

Adams, S. (1959). *Effectiveness of the Youth Authority Special Treatment Program: First interim report* (Research Rep. No. 5). Sacramento: California Department of the Youth Authority.

Adams, S. (1961). *Assessment of the psychiatric treatment program, Phase I* (Research Rep. No. 21). Sacramento: California Department of the Youth Authority.

Adams, S. (1962). The PICO Project. In N. Johnson, L. Sevitz, & M. E. Wolfgang (Eds.), *The sociology of punishment and correction.* New York: Wiley.

Adelson, J., & Gallatin, J. (1983). The adolescent view of crime and justice. In W. S. Laufer & J. M. Day (Eds.), *Personality theory, moral development, and criminal behavior.* Lexington, MA: Lexington.

Adkins, W. R. (1970). Life skills: Structured counseling for the disadvantaged. *Personnel and Guidance Journal, 49,* 108–116.

Agee, V. L. (1979). *Treatment of the violent incorrigible adolescent.* Lexington, MA: Lexington.

Agee, V. L., & McWilliams, B. (1984). The role of group therapy and the therapeutic community in treating the violent juvenile offender. In R. A. Mathias, P. DeMuro, & R. S. Allison (Eds.), *Violent juvenile offenders.* San Francisco: National Council on Crime and Delinquency.

Aichhorn, A. (1925). *Wayward youth.* New York: Viking.

Aichhorn, A. (1949). Some remarks on the psychic structure and social care of a certain type of juvenile delinquent. In *Psychoanalytic study of the child* (Vols. 3–4). New York: International Universities Press.

Akers, R. L. (1985). *Deviant behavior.* Belmont, CA: Wadsworth.

Alexander, F., & Healy, W. (1935). *Roots of crime.* New York: Knopf.

Alexander, J. F. (1973). Defensive and supportive communications in normal and deviant families. *Journal of Consulting and Clinical Psychology, 40,* 223–231.

Alexander, J. F., & Parsons, B. V. (1982). Short-term behavioral intervention with delinquent families: Impact on family process and recidivism. *Journal of Abnormal Psychology, 81,* 219–225.

Alinsky, S. D. (1941). Community analysis and organization. *American Journal of Sociology, 46,* 17–27.

Arbuthnot, J., & Gordon, D. A. (1987). Personality. In H. C. Quay (Ed.), *Handbook of juvenile delinquency.* New York: Wiley.

Argyle, M., Trower, P., & Bryant, B. (1974). Explorations in the treatment of personality disorders and neurosis by social skill training. *British Journal of Medical Psychology, 47,* 63–72.

Aultman, M. G., & Wellford, C. F. (1978). Towards an integrated model of delinquency causation: An empirical analysis. *Sociology and Social Research, 63,* 316–327.

Axelrod, S., & Apache, J. (Eds.). (1982). *The effects of punishment on human behavior.* New York: Academic.

Bahr, S. J. (1979). Family determinants and effects of deviance. In W. R. Burr, R. Hill, F. I. Nye, & I. L. Reiss (Eds.), *Contemporary theories about the family: Research-based theories.* New York: Free Press.

Bailey, J. S., Timbers, G. D., Phillips, E. L., & Wolf, M. M. (1971). Modification of articulation errors of pre-delinquents by their peers. *Journal of Applied Behavior Analysis, 4,* 265–281.

Bandura, A. (1969). *Principles of behavior modification.* New York: Holt, Rinehart & Winston.

Bandura, A. (1973). *Aggression: A social learning analysis.* Englewood Cliffs, NJ: Prentice-Hall.

Bandura, A. (1978). Learning and behavioral theories of aggression. In I. L. Kutash, S. B. Kutash, & L. B. Schlessinger (Eds.), *Violence: Perspectives on murder and aggression.* San Francisco: Jossey-Bass.

Bandura, A. (1986). *Social foundations of thought and action.* Englewood Cliffs, NJ: Prentice-Hall.

Bartollas, C. (1985). *Correctional treatment: Theory and practice.* Englewood Cliffs, NJ: Prentice-Hall.

Barton, C., & Alexander, J. (1981). Functional family therapy. In A. S. Gurman & D. P. Kniskern (Eds.), *Handbook of family therapy.* New York: Brunner/Mazel.

Bassett, J. E., Blanchard, E. B., & Koshland, E. (1975). Applied behavior analysis in a penal setting: Targeting "free world" behaviors. *Behavior Therapy, 6,* 639–648.

Beal, D., & Duckro, P. (1977). Family counseling as an alternative to legal action for the juvenile status offender. *Journal of Marriage and Family Counseling, 3,* 77–81.

Becker, H. S. (1963). *Outsiders: Studies in the sociology of deviance.* Glencoe, IL: Free Press.

Bennett, J. (1981). *Oral history and delinquency: The rhetoric of criminology.* Chicago: University of Chicago Press.

Bernstein, K., & Christiansen, K. (1965). A resocialization experiment with short-term offenders. *Scandinavian Studies in Criminology, 1,* 35–54.

Binder, A. (1987). An historical and theoretical introduction. In H. C. Quay (Ed.), *Handbook of juvenile delinquency.* New York: Wiley.

Black, D., & Reiss, A. J. (1970). Police control of juveniles. *American Sociological Review, 35,* 63–77.

Bogdan, R. C., & Biklen, S. K. (1982). *Qualitative research for education.* Boston: Allyn & Bacon.

Bogdan, R. C., & Taylor, S. J. (1975). *Introduction to qualitative research methods.* New York: Wiley.

Bohman, M., Cloninger, C. R., Sigvardsson, S., & vonKnorring, A. Y. (1982). Predisposition to petty criminality in Swedish adoptees. *Archives of General Psychiatry, 39,* 1233–1241.

Bohman, W. M. (1969). Toward realizing the prevention of mental illness. In L. Bellak & H. Barton (Eds.), *Progress in community mental health* (Vol. 1). New York: Grune & Stratton.

Boston University Training Center in Youth Development. (1966). *Educational counselors: Training for a new definition of after-care of juvenile parolees.* Boston: Boston University Press.

Bostow, D. E., & Bailey, J. B. (1969). Modification of severe disruptive and aggressive behavior using brief time-out and reinforcement procedures. *Journal of Applied Behavior Analysis, 2,* 31–37.

Bowlby, J. (1949). *Why delinquency?* (Report of the Conference on the Scientific Study of Juvenile Delinquency). London: National Association for Mental Health.

Bowman, P. C., & Auerbach, S. M. (1982). Impulsive youthful offenders: A multimodal cognitive behavioral treatment program. *Criminal Justice and Behavior, 9,* 432–454.

Brager, G. A., & Purcell, F. P. (1967). *Community action against poverty.* New Haven, CT: College and University Press.

Brendtro, L. K., Ness, A. E., & Nicolaou, A. W. (1983). Peer-group treatment: Its use and misuse. In L. K. Brendtro & A. E. Ness (Eds.), *Re-educating troubled youth.* New York: Aldine.

Brody, S. R. (1976). *The effectiveness of sentencing—A review of the literature* (Home Office Research Study No. 35). London: Her Majesty's Stationery Office.

Brown, P., & Elliott, R. (1965). Control of aggression in a nursery school class. *Journal of Experimental Child Psychology, 2,* 103–107.

Brown, W. (1983). *The other side of delinquency.* New Brunswick, NJ: Rutgers University Press.

Burchard, J. D., & Barrera, F. (1972). An analysis of timeout and response cost in a programmed environment. *Journal of Applied Behavior Analysis, 5,* 271–282.

Burgess, R. L., & Akers, R. L. (1966). A differential association–reinforcement theory of criminal behavior. *Social Problems, 14,* 128–147.

California Department of the Youth Authority. (1967). *James Marshall Treatment Program.* Unpublished manuscript.

Camp, B. N., & Bash, M. A. (1975). *Think Aloud Program group manual.* Unpublished manuscript, University of Colorado Medical Center, Boulder.

Campbell, M., Cohen, I. L., & Small, A. M. (1982). Drugs in aggressive behavior. *Journal of the American Academy of Child Psychiatry, 21,* 107–117.

Carney, F. J. (1966). *Summary of studies on the derivation of base expectancy categories for predicting recidivism of subjects released from institutions of the Massachusetts Department of Corrections.* Boston: Massachusetts Department of Corrections.

Carney, L. P. (1977). *Probation and parole: Legal and social dimensions.* New York: McGraw-Hill.

Carpenter, P., & Sugrue, D. P. (1984). Psychoeducation in an out-patient setting—Designing a heterogeneous format for a heterogeneous population of juvenile delinquents. *Adolescence, 19,* 113–122.

Center for Studies of Crime and Delinquency. (1973). *Community based correctional program models and practices.* Washington, DC: National Institute of Mental Health.

Chandler, M. (1973). Egocentrism and antisocial behavior: The assessment and training of social perspective-taking skills. *Developmental Psychology, 9,* 326–332.

Christiansen, K. O. (1977). A review of studies of criminality among twins. In S. A. Mednick & K. O. Christiansen (Eds.), *Biosocial bases of criminal behavior.* New York: Wiley.

Christopherson, E. R., Arnold, C. M., Hill, D. W., & Quilitch, H. R. (1972). The home point system: Token reinforcement procedures for application by parents of children with behavior problems. *Journal of Applied Behavior Analysis, 5,* 485–497.

Clark, K. B. (1965). *Dark ghetto: Dilemmas of social power.* New York: Harper & Row.

Clarke, R. V. G. (1977). Psychology and crime. *Bulletin of the British Psychological Society, 30,* 280–283.

Cleckley, H. (1964). *The mask of sanity.* St. Louis: Mosby.

Cloward, R. A., & Ohlin, L. E. (1960). *Delinquency and opportunity: A theory of delinquent gangs.* New York: Free Press.

Cohen, A. K. (1955). *Delinquent boys: The culture of the gang.* Glencoe, IL: Free Press.

Cohen, H. L., & Filipczak, J. A. (1971). *A new learning environment.* San Francisco: Jossey-Bass.

Cohen, L. E., & Land, K. C. (1987). Sociological positivism and the explanation of criminality. In F. R. Gottfredson & T. Hirschi (Eds.), *Positive criminology.* Newbury Park, CA: Sage.

Conger, J. J., & Miller, W. C. (1966). *Personality, social class, and delinquency.* New York: Wiley.

Cook, P. J. (1980). Research in criminal deterrence: Laying the groundwork for the second decade. In N. Morris & M. Tomry (Eds.), *Crime and justice: An annual review of research.* Chicago: University of Chicago Press.

Corning, P. A., & Corning, C. H. (1972). Toward a general theory of violent aggression. *Social Science Information, 11,* 7–13.

Cortes, J. B., & Gatti, F. M. (1972). *Delinquency and crime.* New York: Seminar.

Craft, M., Stephenson, G., & Granger, C. (1964). A controlled trial of authoritarian and self-governing regimes with adolescent psychopaths. *American Journal of Orthopsychiatry, 34,* 543–554.

Crocker, D. (1955). A study of a problem of aggression. *Psychoanalytic Study of the Child, 10,* 300–335.

Cronbach, L. J., & Snow, R. E. (1977). *Aptitudes and instructional methods.* New York: Irvington.

Crowe, R. R. (1975). An adoptive study of psychopathy. In R. R. Fieve, D. Rosenthal, & H. Brill (Eds.), *Genetic research in psychiatry.* Baltimore: Johns Hopkins University Press.

Curry, J. F., Wiencrot, S. I., & Koehler, F. (1984). Family therapy with aggressive and delinquent adolescents. In C. R. Keith (Ed.), *The aggressive adolescent.* New York: Free Press.

Dalgaard, O. S., & Kringlen, E. (1976). A Norwegian twin study of criminality. *British Journal of Criminology, 16,* 213–232.

DeLange, J. M., Lanham, S. L., & Barton, J. A. (1981). Social skills training for juvenile delinquents: Behavioral skill training and cognitive techniques. In D. Upper & S. Ross (Eds.), *Behavioral group therapy, 1981: An annual review* (Vol. 3). Champaign, IL: Research Press.

Deur, J. L., & Parke, P. D. (1970). The effects of inconsistent punishment on aggression in children. *Developmental Psychology, 2,* 403–411.

Dugdale, R. L. (1942). *The Jukes: A study in crime, pauperism, disease, and heredity.* New York: Putnam.

D'Zurilla, T. J., & Goldfried, M. R. (1971). Problem solving and behavior modification. *Journal of Abnormal Psychology, 78,* 107–126.

Edelman, E., & Goldstein, A. P. (1984). Prescriptive relationship levels for juvenile delinquents in a psychotherapy analog. *Aggressive Behavior, 10,* 269–278.

Eissler, K. R. (1950). Ego-psychological implications of the psychoanalytic treatment of delinquents. *Psychoanalytic Study of the Child, 5,* 97–121.

Elardo, P., & Cooper, M. (1977). *AWARE: Activities for social development.* Reading, MA: Addison-Wesley.

Elliott, D. S., Ageton, S. S., & Canter, R. J. (1979). An integrated theoretical perspective on juvenile delinquency. *Journal of Research in Crime and Delinquency, 16,* 3–27.

Elliott, D. S., Huizenga, D., & Ageton, S. S. (1985). *Explaining delinquency and drug use.* Beverly Hills, CA: Sage.

Elliott, D. S., & Voss, H. L. (1974). *Delinquency and dropout.* Toronto: Lexington.

Ellis, H. (1914). *The criminal.* London: Scott.

Ellis, L. (1987). Neurohormonal bases of varying tendencies to learn delinquent and criminal behavior. In C. J. Braukmann & E. K. Morris (Eds.), *Behavioral approaches to crime and delinquency.* New York: Plenum.

Empey, L. T. (1969). Contemporary programs for convicted juvenile offenders: Problems of theory, practice and research. In D. J. Mulvihill & M. M. Tremis (Eds.), *Crimes of violence* (Vol. 13). Washington, DC: U. S. Government Printing Office.

Empey, L. T., & Erickson, M. L. (1972). *The Provo experiment: Evaluating community control of delinquency.* Lexington, MA: Lexington.

Epps, P., & Parnell, R. W. (1952). Physique and temperament of women delinquents compared with women undergraduates. *British Journal of Medical Psychology, 25,* 249–255.

Everett, C. (1976). Family assessment and intervention for early adolescent problems. *Journal of Marriage and Family Counseling, 2,* 155–165.

Eysenck, H. J. (1977). *Crime and personality.* London: Routledge & Kegan Paul.

Fagan, J. A., & Hartstone, E. (1984). Strategic planning in juvenile justice—Defining the toughest kids. In R. Q. Mathias, P. DeMuro, & R. S. Allinson (Eds.), *Violent juvenile offenders.* San Francisco: National Council on Crime and Delinquency.

Farrington, D. P., Gundry, G., & West, D. J. (1975). The familial transmission of criminality. *Medicine, Science and the Law, 15,* 177–186.

Feindler, E. L., & Ecton, R. (1986). *Anger control training.* New York: Pergamon.

Feindler, E. L., Marriott, S. A., & Iwata, M. (1984). Group anger control training for junior high school delinquents. *Cognitive Therapy and Research, 8,* 299–311.

Feistman, E. G. (1966). *Comparative analysis of the Willowbrook-Harbor Intensive Services Program* (Research Rep. No. 28). Los Angeles: Los Angeles County Probation Department.

Feldman, M. P. (1977). *Criminal behavior: A psychological analysis.* London: Wiley.

Feldman, R. A., Caplinger, T. E., & Wodarski, J. S. (1983). *The St. Louis conundrum: The effective treatment of antisocial youth.* Englewood Cliffs, NJ: Prentice-Hall.

Ferdun, G. S. (1974). Educational research. In K. Griffiths (Ed.), *A review of accumulated research in the California Youth Authority.* Sacramento: California Department of the Youth Authority.

Feshbach, S. (1970). Aggression. In P. H. Mussen (Ed.), *Carmichael's manual of child psychology* (Vol. 2). New York: Wiley.

Figgie International. (1988). *The Figgie Report Part VI. The business of crime: The criminal perspective.* Richmond, VA: Author.

Filipczak, J. A., Friedman, R. M., & Reese, S. C. (1979). PREP: Educational programming to prevent juvenile problems. In J. S. Stumphauzer (Ed.), *Progress in behavior therapy with delinquents.* Springfield, IL: Charles C Thomas.

Finckenauer, J. O. (1982). *Scared Straight! and the panacea phenomenon.* Englewood Cliffs, NJ: Prentice-Hall.

Fleischman, M. J. (1982). Social learning interventions for aggressive children: From the laboratory to the real world. *The Behavior Therapist, 5,* 55–58.

Fleischman, M. J., & Szykula, S. A. (1981). A community setting replication of a social learning treatment for aggressive children. *Behavior Therapy, 12,* 115–122.

Fo, W., & O'Donnell, C. (1974). The buddy system: Relationship and contingency conditions in a community intervention program for youth with nonprofessionals as behavior change agents. *Journal of Consulting and Clinical Psychology, 42,* 163–168.

Fo, W., & O'Donnell, C. (1975). The buddy system: Effect of community intervention on delinquent offenses. *Behavior Therapy, 6,* 522–524.

Forehand, R., Wells, K. C., & Griest, D. L. (1980). An examination of the social validity of parent training programs. *Behavior Therapy, 11,* 488–502.

Fox, F. L. (1981). The family and the ex-offender: Potential for rehabilitation. In S. E. Martin, L. B. Sechrest, & R. Redner (Eds.), *New directions in the rehabilitation of criminal offenders.* Washington, DC: National Academy Press.

Foxx, C. L., Foxx, R. M., Jones, J. R., & Kiely, D. (1980). Twenty-four-hour social isolation: A program for reducing the aggressive behavior of a psychotic-like retarded adult. *Behavior Modification, 4,* 130–144.

Foxx, R. M., & Azrin, N. H. (1972). Restitution: A method of eliminating aggressive-disruptive behavior of retarded and brain-damaged patients. *Behaviour Research and Therapy, 10,* 15–27.

Freud, S. (1961). *The complete works of Sigmund Freud.* London: Hogarth.

Friedlander, K. (1947). *The psychoanalytic approach to juvenile delinquency.* New York: International Universities Press.

Funke, L., & Booth, J. E. (Eds.). (1961). *Actors talk about acting.* New York: Discus.

Furnham, A. F. (1988). *Lay theories: Everyday understanding of problems in the social sciences.* New York: Pergamon.

Furniss, J. (1964). *Peer reinforcement of behavior in an institution for delinquent girls.* Unpublished master's thesis, Oregon State University, Corvallis.

Garrett, C. J. (1985). Effects of residential treatment on adjudicated delinquents: A meta-analysis. *Journal of Research on Crime and Delinquency, 22,* 287–308.

Garrity, D. (1956). *The effects of length of incarceration upon parole adjustment and estimation of optimum sentence.* Unpublished doctoral dissertation, University of Washington, Seattle.

Gensheimer, L. K., Mayer, J. P., Gottschalk, R., & Davidson, W. S. (1986). Diverting youth from the juvenile justice system: A meta-analysis of intervention efficacy. In S. J. Apter & A. P. Goldstein (Eds.), *Youth violence.* New York: Pergamon.

Gibbens, T. C. (1963). *Psychiatric studies of Borstal lads.* London: Oxford University Press.

Gibbs, J. C. (1986). *Small group sociomoral treatment programs: Dilemmas for use with conduct-disordered or antisocial adolescents or preadolescents.* Unpublished manuscript, Ohio State University, Columbus.

Gittleman-Klein, R., Spitzer, R. L., & Cantwell, D. (1978). Diagnostic classification and psychopharmacological indications. In J. S. Werry (Ed.), *Pediatric psychopharmacology: The use of behavior modifying drugs in children.* New York: Brunner/Mazel.

Gladstone, H. P. (1962). A study of techniques of psychotherapy with youthful offenders. *Psychiatry, 25,* 147–159.

Glaser, B. G. (1987). The constant comparative method of qualitative analysis. In G. J. McCall & J. L. Simmons (Eds.), *Issues in participant observation: A text and reader.* Reading, MA: Addison-Wesley.

Glaser, D. (1956). Criminality theories and behavioral images. In D. R. Cressey & D. A. Ward (Eds.), *Delinquency, crime, and social process.* New York: Harper & Row.

Glaser, D. (1973, November). The state of the art of criminal justice evaluation. Paper presented at the meeting of the Association for Criminal Justice Research, Los Angeles.

Glaser, W. (1969). *Schools without failure.* New York: Harper & Row.

Glover, E. (1944). The diagnosis and treatment of delinquency. In L. Radzinowicz & J. W. C. Turner (Eds.), *Mental abnormality and crime.* London: Macmillan.

Glover, E. (1960). *The roots of crime.* New York: International Universities Press.

Glueck, S., & Glueck, E. T. (1950). *Unraveling juvenile delinquency.* Cambridge, MA: Harvard University Press.

Goddard, H. H. (1916). *The Kallikak family: A study in the heredity of feeblemindedness.* New York: Macmillan.

Goins, S. (1977). The serious or violent juvenile offender—Is there a treatment response? In *The serious juvenile offender: Proceedings of a national symposium.* Washington, DC: U. S. Government Printing Office.

Gold, M. (1963). *Status forces in delinquent boys.* Ann Arbor: University of Michigan Press.

Gold, M. (1970). *Delinquent behavior in an American city.* Belmont, CA: Brooks/Cole.

Goldstein, A. P. (Ed.). (1978). *Prescriptions for child mental health and education.* New York: Pergamon.

Goldstein, A. P., Apter, S. J., & Harootunian, B. (1984). *School violence.* Englewood Cliffs, NJ: Prentice-Hall.

Goldstein, A. P., & Glick, B. (1987). *Aggression Replacement Training: A comprehensive intervention for aggressive youth.* Champaign, IL: Research Press.

Goldstein, A. P., Glick, B., Irwin, M. J., Pask-McCartney, C., & Rubama, I. (1989). *Reducing delinquency: Intervention in the community.* New York: Pergamon.

Goldstein, A. P., & Keller, H. (1987). *Aggressive behavior: Assessment and intervention.* New York: Pergamon.

Goldstein, A. P., Sprafkin, R. P., Gershaw, N. J., & Klein, P. (1980). *Skillstreaming the adolescent: A structured learning approach to teaching prosocial skills.* Champaign, IL: Research Press.

Goldstein, A. P., & Stein, N. (1976). *Prescriptive psychotherapies.* New York: Pergamon.

Gordon, D. A., & Arbuthnot, J. (1987). Individual, group, and family intervention. In H. C. Quay (Ed.), *Handbook of juvenile delinquency.* New York: Wiley.

Goring, C. (1913). *The English convict: A statistical study.* London: Darling & Son.

Gottschalk, R., Davidson, W. S., Mayer, J., & Gensheimer, L. K., (1987). Behavioral approaches with juvenile offenders: A meta-analysis of long-term treatment efficacy. In E. K. Morris & C. J. Braukmann (Eds.), *Behavioral approaches to crime and delinquency.* New York: Plenum.

Grant, J., & Grant, M. Q. (1959). A group dynamics approach to the treatment of nonconformists in the navy. *Annals of the American Academy of Political and Social Science, 322,* 126–133.

Greenwood, P. W. (1986). *Intervention strategies for chronic juvenile offenders.* New York: Greenwood.

Grendreau, P., & Ross, R. R. (1987). Revivication of rehabilitation: Evidence from the 1980s. *Justice Quarterly, 4,* 349–397.

Gutterman, E. S. (1963). *Effects of short-term psychiatric treatment* (Research Rep. No. 36). Sacramento: California Department of the Youth Authority.

Hackler, J. C. (1965). Boys, blisters, and behavior: The impact of a work program in an urban control area. *Journal of Research in Crime and Delinquency, 3*, 155–164.

Hall, R. V., Axelrod, S., Foundopoulos, M., Shellman, J., Campbell, R. S., & Cranston, S. S. (1971). The effective use of punishment to modify behavior in the classroom. *Education Technology, 11*, 24–26.

Hammersley, M., & Atkinson, P. (1983). *Ethnography: Principles in practice.* London: Tavistock.

Hamparian, D. M., Schuster, R., Dinitz, S., & Conrad, J. P. (1978). *The violent few: A study of dangerous juvenile offenders.* Lexington, MA: Lexington.

Hanson, B., Beschner, G., Walters, J. M., & Bovelle, E. (1985). *Life with heroin: Voices from the inner city.* Lexington, MA: Heath.

Hargardine, J. E. (1968). *The Attention Homes of Boulder, Colorado.* Washington, DC: U. S. Department of Health, Education, and Welfare, Juvenile Delinquency and Youth Development Office.

Harlow, E., Weber, J. R., & Wilkins, L. T. (1971). *Community based correctional program models and practices.* Washington, DC: National Institute of Mental Health, Center for Studies of Crime and Delinquency.

Harrison, R. M., & Mueller, P. (1964). *Clue hunting about group counseling and parole outcome.* Sacramento: California Department of Corrections.

Hawkins, J. D., & Weis, J. G. (1985). The social development model: An integrated approach to delinquency prevention. *Journal of Primary Prevention, 6*, 73–97.

Hawkins, R., & Tiedemann, G. (1975). *The creation of deviance: Interpersonal and organizational determinants.* Columbus, OH: Merrill.

Healy, W. (1915). *The individual delinquent.* Boston: Little, Brown.

Healy, W., & Bronner, A. (1936). *New light on delinquency and its treatment.* New Haven, CT: Yale University Press.

Heaton, R. C., & Safer, D. J. (1982). Secondary school outcome following a junior high school behavioral program. *Behavior Therapy, 13*, 226–231.

Henderson, C. R. (1910). *Prison reform and criminal law.* New York: Charities Publication Committee.

Hewitt, J. P. (1970). *Social stratification and deviant behavior.* New York: Random House.

Himelhoch, S. (1965). Delinquency and opportunity: An end and a beginning of theory. In L. Gouldner & M. Miller (Eds.), *Applied sociology.* New York: Free Press.

Hindelang, M. (1972). The relationship of self-reported delinquency to scales of the CPI and the MMPI. *Journal of Criminal Law, Criminology, and Police Science, 63,* 75–81.

Hirschi, T. (1969). *Causes of delinquency.* Berkeley: University of California Press.

Hogan, R., & Jones, W. H. (1983). A role-theoretical model of criminal conduct. In W. S. Laufer & J. M. Day (Eds.), *Personality theory, moral development, and criminal behavior.* Lexington, MA: Lexington.

Hollin, C. R. (1989). *Cognitive-behavioral interventions with young offenders.* New York: Pergamon.

Hollin, C. R., Huff, G. J., Clarkson, F., & Edmondson, A. C. (1986). Social skills training with young offenders in a Borstal: An evaluative study. *Journal of Community Psychology, 14,* 289–299.

Hoskins, R. G. (1941). *Endocrinology.* New York: Norton.

Hudson, C. H. (1973). *Summary report: An experimental study of the differential effects of parole supervision for a group of adolescent boys and girls.* Minneapolis: Minnesota Department of Corrections.

Hunt, D. E. (1972). Matching models for teacher training. In B. R. Joyce & M. Weil (Eds.), *Perspectives for reform in teacher education.* Englewood Cliffs, NJ: Prentice-Hall.

Ingram, G. L., Gerard, R. E., Quay, H. C., & Levinson, R. B. (1970). An experimental program for the psychopathic delinquent: Looking in the "correctional wastebasket." *Journal of Research in Crime and Delinquency, 7,* 24–30.

Irwin, J. (1970). *The felon.* Englewood Cliffs, NJ: Prentice-Hall.

Jacobson, F., & McGee, E. (1965). *Englewood Project: Re-education: A radial correction of incarcerated youth.* Unpublished manuscript, Englewood, CO.

Jennings, W. S., Kilkenny, R., & Kohlberg, L. (1983). Moral development theory and practice for youthful and adult offenders. In W. S. Laufer & J. M. Day (Eds.), *Personality theory, moral development, and criminal behavior.* Lexington, MA: Lexington.

Jesness, C. (1965). *The Fricot Ranch Study.* Sacramento, CA: California Department of the Youth Authority.

Jesness, C., Allison, T., McCormick, R., Wedge, R., & Young, M. (1975). *Cooperative Behavior Demonstration Project.* Sacramento: California Department of the Youth Authority.

Johnson, A. M. (1949). Sanctions for super-ego lacunae. In K. R. Eissler (Ed.), *Searchlights on delinquency.* New York: International Universities Press.

Johnson, A. M. (1959). Juvenile delinquency. In S. Arieti (Ed.), *American handbook of psychiatry.* New York: Basic.

Johnson, A. M., & Szurek, S. A. (1952). The genesis of antisocial acting out in children and adults. *Psychoanalytic Quarterly, 21,* 323–343.

Johnson, B. M. (1965). The "failure" of a parole research project. *California Youth Authority Quarterly, 18,* 35–39.

Johnson, F. (1975). Family therapy with families having delinquent offspring. *Journal of Family Counseling, 3,* 32–37.

Johnson, R. E. (1979). *Juvenile delinquency and its origins.* Cambridge: Cambridge University Press.

Jones, A. P. (1988). *Prison boot camps.* Washington, DC: U. S. General Accounting Office.

Jones, F. H., & Miller, W. H. (1974). The effective use of negative attention for reducing group disruption in special elementary school classrooms. *The Psychological Record, 24,* 435–448.

Jones, M. (1953). *The therapeutic community.* New York: Basic.

Jurjevich, R. M. (1968). *No water in my cup: Experiences and a controlled study of psychotherapy of delinquent girls.* New York: Libra.

Kazdin, A. E. (1985). *Treatment of antisocial behavior in children and adolescents.* Homewood, IL: Dorsey.

Kazdin, A. E. (1987). *Conduct disorders in childhood and adolescence.* Newbury Park, CA: Sage.

Keith, C. R. (Ed.). (1984a). *The aggressive adolescent.* New York: Free Press.

Keith, C. R. (1984b). Individual psychotherapy and psychoanalysis with the aggressive adolescent: A historical review. In C. R. Keith (Ed.), *The aggressive adolescent.* New York: Free Press.

Keller, F. S. (1966). A personal course in psychology. In R. Ulrich, T. Stachnik, & J. Mabry (Eds.), *Control of human behavior.* Glenview, IL: Scott, Foresman.

Kelly, F. J., & Baer, D. J. (1968). *Outward Bound schools as an alternative to institutionalization for adolescent delinquent boys.* Boston: Fandel.

Kentucky Child Welfare Research Foundation. (1967). *Community rehabilitation of the younger delinquent boy: Parkland Non-Residential Group Center.* Washington, DC: U. S. Department of Health, Education, and Welfare.

Kiesler, D. J. (1969). A grid model for theory and research. In L. D. Eron & R. Callahan (Eds.), *The relation of theory to practice in psychotherapy.* Chicago: Aldine.

Kitwood, T. (1980). *Disclosures to a stranger: Adolescent values in an advanced industrial society.* London: Routledge & Kegan Paul.

Klausmeier, H. J., Rossmiller, R. A., & Sailey, M. (1977). *Individually guided elementary education.* New York: Academic.

Knapp, D., & Polk, K. (1971). *Scouting the War on Poverty: Social reform politics in the Kennedy administration.* Lexington, MA: Lexington.

Knight, D. (1969). *The Marshall Program, assessment of a short-term institutional treatment program* (Research Rep. No. 56). Sacramento: California Department of the Youth Authority.

Knight, D. (1970). *The Marshall Program, assessment of a short-term institutional treatment program. Part II: Amenability to confrontive peer-group treatment* (Research Rep. No. 59). Sacramento: California Department of the Youth Authority.

Kobrin, S. (1959). The Chicago Area Project: A twenty-five-year assessment. *Annals of the American Academy of Political and Social Science, 322,* 136–151.

Kobrin, S., & Klein, M. W. (1983). *Community treatment of juvenile offenders: The DSO experiments.* Beverly Hills, CA: Sage.

Kohlberg, L. (1969). Stage and sequence: The cognitive-developmental approach to socialization. In D. A. Goslin (Ed.), *Handbook of socialization theory and research.* Chicago: Rand McNally.

Kohlberg, L. (Ed.). (1973). *Collected papers in moral development and moral education.* Cambridge, MA: Harvard University, Center for Moral Education.

Kornhauser, R. (1978). *Social sources of delinquency.* Chicago: University of Chicago Press.

Kozeny, E. (1962). Experimentelle Untersuchungen zur Ausdruck-kundemittel photographisch-statistischer Methode. [Experimental research on the use of the photographic-statistical method in the study of physiognomic expression]. *Archives für die Gesamte Psychologie, 114,* 55–71.

Krantz, H. (1936). *Lebensschicksale krimineller Zwillinge.* [Life patterns of criminal twins]. Berlin: Springer-Verlag.

Kratcoski, P. C., & Kratcoski, M. A. (1975). Changing patterns in the delinquent activities of boys and girls: A self-reported delinquency analysis. *Adolescence, 10,* 83–91.

Kraus, J. (1974). The deterrent effect of fines and probation on male juvenile offenders. *Australian and New Zealand Journal of Criminology, 7,* 231–240.

Krohn, M. D., Massey, J. L., & Skinner, W. F. (1987). A sociological theory of crime and delinquency: Social learning theory. In C. J. Braukmann & E. K. Morris (Eds.), *Behavioral approaches to crime and delinquency.* New York: Plenum.

Kulik, J. A., Stein, K. B., & Sarbin, T. R. (1968). Disclosure of delinquent behavior under conditions of anonymity and nonanonymity. *Journal of Consulting and Clinical Psychology, 32,* 506–509.

Lang, R. (1988). *Potential social impacts of Halton's landfill on communities at site F in Burlington.* Toronto: Lang.

Lange, J. (1928). *Crime as destiny.* London: George Allen & Unwin.

Laufer, W. S., & Day, J. M. (Eds.). (1983). *Personality theory, moral development, and criminal behavior.* Lexington, MA: Lexington.

Lavin, G. K., Trabka, S., & Kahn, E. M. (1984). Group therapy with aggressive and delinquent adolescents. In C. R. Keith (Ed.), *The aggressive adolescent.* New York: Free Press.

Lemert, E. M. (1967). *Human deviance, social problems, and social control.* Englewood Cliffs, NJ: Prentice-Hall.

Levinson, R. B., & Kitchener, H. L. (1964). *Demonstration counseling project.* Washington, DC: National Training School for Boys.

Levy, D. M. (1932). On the problem of delinquency. *American Journal of Orthopsychiatry, 2,* 197–207.

Lindblom, C. E., & Cohen, D. K. (1929). *Usable knowledge: Social science and social problem solving.* New Haven, CT: Yale University Press.

Linden, R. (1978). Myths of middle-class delinquency. *Youth and Society, 9,* 407–432.

Lindgren, J. G. (1987). Social policy and the prevention of delinquency. In J. D. Burchard & N. S. Burchard (Eds.), *Prevention of delinquent behavior.* Newbury Park, CA: Sage.

Little, V. L., & Kendall, D. C. (1979). Cognitive-behavioral intervention with delinquents: Problem solving, role taking and self-control. In P. C. Kendall & S. D. Hollon (Eds.), *Cognitive-behavioral interventions: Theory, research, and procedures.* New York: Academic.

Litwack, S. E. (1976). *The helper therapy principle as a therapeutic tool: Structured learning therapy with adolescents.* Unpublished doctoral dissertation, Syracuse University, Syracuse, NY.

Loeber, R., & Dishion, T. (1983). Early predictors of male delinquency: A review. *Psychological Bulletin, 94,* 68–99.

Lombroso, C. (1911). *Crime, its causes and remedies.* Boston: Little, Brown.

Lundman, R. J. (1984). *Prevention and control of delinquency.* New York: Oxford University Press.

Lundman, R. J., Sykes, R. E., & Clark, J. P. (1978). Police control of juveniles: A replication. *Journal of Research in Crime and Delinquency, 15,* 74–91.

Magaro, P. A. (1969). A prescriptive treatment model based on social class and premorbid adjustment. *Psychotherapy: Theory, Research, and Practice, 6,* 57–70.

Maher, B. (1966). The delinquent's perception of the law and the community. In S. Wheeler (Ed.), *Controlling delinquents.* New York: Wiley.

Maltz, M. D. (1984). *Recidivism.* New York: Academic.

Manocchio, A. J., & Dunn, J. (1970). *The time game: Two views of a prison.* Newbury Park, CA: Sage.

Mark, V. H., & Erwin, F. R. (1970). *Violence and the brain.* New York: Harper & Row.

Marris, P., & Rein, M. (1969). *Dilemmas of social reform: Poverty and community action in the United States.* New York: Atherton.

Martin, P. L., & Foxx, R. M. (1973). Victim control of the aggression of an institutionalized retardate. *Journal of Behavior Therapy and Experimental Psychiatry, 4,* 161–165.

Martin, S. E., Sechrest, L. B., & Redner, R. (1981). *New directions in the rehabilitation of criminal offenders.* Washington, DC: National Academy.

Martinson, R. (1974, Spring). What works? Questions and answers about prison reform. *The Public Interest,* pp. 22–54.

Matson, J. L., Stephens, R. M., & Horne, A. M. (1978). Overcorrection and extinction-reinforcement as rapid methods of eliminating the disruptive behaviors of relatively normal children. *Behavioral Engineering, 4,* 89–94.

Matza, D. (1964). *Delinquency and drift.* New York: Wiley.

McCord, W., & McCord, J. (1959). *Origins of crime: A new evaluation of the Cambridge-Somerville study.* New York: Columbia University Press.

McCord, W., & McCord, J. (1964). *The psychopath: An essay on the criminal mind.* Princeton, NJ: Van Nostrand Reinhold.

McCorkle, L., Elias, A., & Bixby, F. (1958). *The Highfields story: A unique experiment in the treatment of juvenile delinquency.* New York: Holt.

McCullough, J. P., Huntsinger, G. M., & Nay, W. R. (1977). Case study: Self-control treatment of aggression in a 16-year-old male. *Journal of Consulting and Clinical Psychology, 45,* 322–331.

Mead, G. H. (1934). *Mind, self and society.* Chicago: University of Chicago Press.

Mednick, S. A. (1977). A bio-social theory of the learning of law-abiding behavior. In S. A. Mednick & K. O. Christiansen (Eds.), *Biosocial bases of criminal behavior.* New York: Wiley.

Megargee, E. I., & Bohn, M. J., Jr. (1979). *Classifying criminal offenders: A new system based on the MMPI*. Beverly Hills, CA: Sage.

Meier, R. (1976). The new criminology: Continuity in criminological theory. *Journal of Criminal Law and Criminology, 67*, 461–469.

Meltzer, M. (1984). *The Black Americans: A history in their own words, 1619–1983*. New York: Harper & Row.

Mercer, M., & Renda, I. (1985). *Taking care*. New York: Interstate Children's Consortium.

Merrill-Palmer Institute. (1971). *The Detroit Foster Homes Project*. Unpublished manuscript, Detroit, MI.

Merton, R. K. (1938). Social structure and anomie. *American Sociological Review, 3*, 672–682.

Merton, R. K. (1957). *Social theory and social structure*. New York: Free Press.

Metfessel, M., & Lovell, C. (1942). Recent literature on individual correlates of crime. *Psychological Bulletin, 39*, 133–142.

Miller, W. B. (1958). Lower class culture as a generating milieu of gang delinquency. *Journal of Social Issues, 14*, 5–19.

Miller, W. B. (1962). The impact of a total community delinquency control project. *Social Problems, 10*, 168–191.

Molof, M. J. (1967). *Forestry camp study: Comparison of recidivism rates of camp-eligible boys randomly assigned to camp and to institutional programs* (Research Rep. No. 53). Sacramento: California Department of the Youth Authority.

Monahan, J. (1981). *The clinical prediction of violent behavior*. Rockville, MD: National Institute of Mental Health.

Monroe, R. (1970). *Episodic behavioral disorder: A psychodynamic and neurological analysis*. Cambridge, MA: Harvard University Press.

Monroe, S., & Goldman, P. (1988). *Brothers: Black and poor—A true story of courage and survival*. New York: Morrow.

Montagu, A. (1941). The biologist looks at crime. *The Annals, 218*, 53–55.

Morris, E. K., & Braukmann, C. J. (1987). *Behavioral approaches to crime and delinquency*. New York: Plenum.

Mulvey, E. P., & LaRosa, J. F. (1986). Delinquency cessation and adolescent development: Preliminary data. *American Journal of Orthopsychiatry, 56*, 212–224.

National Institute of Law Enforcement and Criminal Justice. (1977). *Project New Pride*. Washington, DC: U. S. Government Printing Office.

Nettler, G. (1974). *Explaining crime*. New York: McGraw-Hill.

Nietzel, M. T. (1979). *Crime and its modification.* New York: Pergamon.

Nietzel, M. T., & Himelein, M. J. (1987). Probation and parole. In E. K. Morris & C. J. Braukmann (Eds.), *Behavioral approaches to crime and delinquency.* New York: Plenum.

Northern California Service League. (1968). *Final report of the San Francisco Rehabilitation Project for Offenders.* San Francisco: Author.

Novaco, R. W. (1975). *Anger control: The development and evaluation of an experimental treatment.* Lexington, MA: Heath.

Nye, F. I. (1958). *Family relationships and delinquent behavior.* New York: Wiley.

O'dell, B. N. (1974, April). Accelerating entry into the opportunity structure. A sociologically based treatment for delinquent youth. *Sociology and Social Research,* pp. 7–14.

O'Leary, K. D., & Becker, W. C. (1967). Behavior modification of an adjustment class: A token reinforcement program. *Exceptional Children, 33,* 637–642.

O'Leary, K. D., Kaufman, K. F., Kass, R. E., & Drabman, R. S. (1970). The effects of loud and soft reprimands on the behavior of disruptive students. *Exceptional Children, 37,* 145–155.

Osborn, S. G., & West, D. J. (1979). Conviction records of fathers and sons compared. *British Journal of Criminology, 19,* 120–133.

Palmer, T. B. (1973). Matching worker and client in corrections. *Social Work, 18,* 95–103.

Palmer, T. B. (1975). Martinson revisited. *Journal of Research in Crime and Delinquency, 12,* 133–152.

Parsons, B. V., & Alexander, J. F. (1973). Short-term family intervention: A therapy outcome study. *Journal of Consulting and Clinical Psychology, 41,* 195–201.

Patterson, G. R. (1963). *The peer group as delinquency reinforcement agent.* Unpublished research report, University of Oregon, Child Research Laboratory.

Patterson, G. R. (1971). Behavioral intervention procedures in the classroom and in the home. In A. E. Bergin & S. L. Garfield (Eds.), *Handbook of psychotherapy and behavior change.* New York: Wiley.

Patterson, G. R. (1974). Interventions for boys with conduct problems: Multiple settings, treatments, and criteria. *Journal of Consulting and Clinical Psychology, 42,* 471–481.

Patterson, G. R. (1976). The aggressive child: Victim and architect of a coercive system. In L. A. Hamerlynck, L. C. Handy, & E. J. Mash

(Eds.), *Behavior modification and families: Theory and research.* New York: Brunner/Mazel.

Patterson, G. R. (1979). Treatment for children with conduct problems: A review of outcome studies. In S. Feshbach & A. Fraczek (Eds.), *Aggression and behavior change: Biological and social processes.* New York: Praeger.

Patterson, G. R. (1982). *Coercive family process.* Eugene, OR: Castalia.

Patterson, G. R., Cobb, J. A., & Ray, R. S. (1973). A social engineering technology for retraining the families of aggressive boys. In H. E. Adams & I. P. Unikel (Eds.), *Issues and trends in behavior therapy.* Springfield, IL: Charles C Thomas.

Patterson, G. R., & Fleischman, M. J. (1979). Maintenance of treatment effects: Some considerations concerning family systems and follow-up data. *Behavior Therapy, 10,* 168–185.

Patterson, G. R., Reid, J. G., Jones, R. R., & Conger, R. E. (1975). *A social learning approach to family intervention.* Eugene OR: Castalia.

Pekkanen, J. (1988). *M.D., Doctors talk about themselves.* New York: Delacorte.

Phillips, E. L. (1968). Achievement Place: Token reinforcement procedures in a home-style rehabilitation setting for pre-delinquent boys. *Journal of Applied Behavior Analysis, 7,* 207–215.

Piliavin, I., & Briar, S. (1964). Police encounters with juveniles. *American Journal of Sociology, 70,* 206–214.

Pilnick, S. (1967). *Collegefields: From delinquency to freedom.* Newark, NJ: Newark State College.

Platt, J. J., & Prout, M. F. (1987). Cognitive-behavioral theory and interventions for crime and delinquency. In E. K. Morris & C. J. Braukmann (Eds.), *Behavioral approaches to crime and delinquency.* New York: Plenum.

Pollock, V., Mednick, S. A., & Gabrielli, W. F. (1983). Crime causation: Biological theories. In S. H. Kadish (Ed.), *Encyclopedia of crime and justice* (Vol. 1). New York: Free Press.

Pond, E. (1970). *The Los Angeles Community Delinquency Control Project: An experiment in the rehabilitation of delinquents in an urban community* (Research Rep. No. 60). Sacramento: California Department of the Youth Authority.

Post, G. C., Hicks, R. A., & Monfort, M. F. (1968). Day care program for delinquents: A new treatment approach. *Crime and Delinquency, 14,* 353–359.

Pottherst, K. E., & Gabriel, M. (1972). *The peer group as a treatment tool in a probation department girls' residential treatment center.* New York: Brunner/Mazel.

President's Commission on Law Enforcement and Administration of Justice. (1967). *Juvenile delinquency and youth crime.* Washington, DC: U. S. Government Printing Office.

Quay, H. C. (1965). Psychopathic personality as pathological stimulation-seeking. *American Journal of Psychiatry, 122,* 180–183.

Quinney, R. (1974). *Critique of legal order: Crime control in capitalist society.* Boston: Little, Brown.

Rabinowitz, C. (1969). Therapy for underprivileged delinquent families. In O. Pollock & A. Friedman (Eds.), *Family dynamics and female sexual delinquency.* Palo Alto, CA: Science and Behavior Books.

Reckless, W. E. (1961). *The crime problem.* New York: Appleton-Century-Crofts.

Reckless, W. E., & Dinitz, S. (1972). *Prevention of juvenile delinquency—An experiment.* Columbus: Ohio State University Press.

Redl, F. (1945). The psychology of gang formation and the treatment of juvenile delinquents. In *Psychoanalytic study of the child* (Vol. 1). New York: International Universities Press.

Redner, R., Snellman, L., & Davidson, W. S. (1983). Juvenile delinquency. In R. J. Morris & T. R. Kratochwill (Eds.), *The practice of child therapy.* New York: Pergamon.

Reiss, A. J., Jr., & Rhodes, A. L. (1964). An empirical test of differential association theory. *Journal of Research in Crime and Delinquency, 1,* 13–17.

Roberts, H. B. (1987). *The inner world of the Black juvenile delinquent.* Hillsdale, NJ: Erlbaum.

Robins, L., West, P. A., & Herjanic, B. L. (1975). Arrests and delinquency in two generations: A study of black urban families and their children. *Journal of Child Psychology and Psychiatry, 16,* 125–140.

Robins, L. N., & Lewis, R. G. (1966). The role of the antisocial family in school completion and delinquency: A three-generation study. *Sociological Quarterly, 7,* 500–514.

Romig, D. A. (1978). *Justice for our children: An examination of juvenile delinquency rehabilitation programs.* Lexington, MA: Lexington.

Rosenthal, D. (1970a). *Genetics of psychopathology.* New York: McGraw-Hill.

Rosenthal, D. (1970b). *Genetic theory and abnormal behavior.* New York: McGraw-Hill.

Rosenthal, P., Moestetler, S., Wells, J., & Rolland, R. (1974). Family therapy and multiproblem, multichildren families in a court clinic setting. *Journal of the American Academy of Child Psychiatry, 13*, 126–142.

Ross, R. R., & Fabiano, E. A. (1985). *Time to think: A cognitive model of delinquency prevention and offender rehabilitation.* Johnson City, TN: Institute of Social Sciences and Arts.

Ruben, M. (1957). Delinquency, a defense against loss of objects and reality. *Psychoanalytic Study of the Child, 12*, 335–349.

Rutter, M. (1971). Parent-child separation: Psychological effects on the child. *Journal of Child Psychology and Psychiatry, 12*, 233–260.

Rutter, M., & Giller, H. (1983). *Juvenile delinquency: Trends and perspectives.* New York: Guilford.

San Diego County Probation Department. (1971). *Research and evaluation of the first year of operations of the San Diego County Juvenile Narcotics Project.* San Diego: Author.

Sarason, I. J., & Ganzer, V. J. (1973). Modeling and group discussion in the rehabilitation of juvenile delinquents. *Journal of Counseling Psychology, 20*, 442–449.

Sawin, D. B., & Parks, R. D. (1979). The effects of interagent inconsistent discipline on children's aggressive behavior. *Journal of Experimental Child Psychology, 28*, 528–535.

Schatzman, L., & Strauss, A. L. (1973). *Field research.* Englewood Cliffs, NJ: Prentice-Hall.

Schlapp, M. G., & Smith, E. H. (1928). *The new criminology.* New York: Boni & Liveright.

Schneider, P. R., Griffith, W. R., & Schneider, A. L. (1982). Juvenile restitution as a sole sanction or condition of probation: An empirical analysis. *Journal of Research in Crime and Delinquency, 19*, 47–65.

Schuessler, K. F., & Cressey, D. R. (1950). Personality characteristics of criminals. *American Journal of Sociology, 55*, 476–484.

Schur, E. (1971). *Labeling deviant behavior: Its sociological implications.* New York: Random House.

Schwitzgebel, R. L. (1967). Short term operant conditioning of adolescent offenders on socially relevant variables. *Journal of Abnormal Psychology, 72*, 134–142.

Schwitzgebel, R. L., & Kolb, D. A. (1964). Inducing behavior change in adolescent delinquents. *Behaviour Research and Therapy, 1*, 297–304.

Sealy, A., & Banks, C. (1971). Social maturity, training, experience, and recidivism amongst British borstal boys. *British Journal of Criminology, 11*, 245–264.

Seckel, J. (1975). *Assessment of Preston Family Drug Treatment Project.* Sacramento: California Department of the Youth Authority.

Shannon, L. W. (1988). *Criminal career continuity.* New York: Human Sciences.

Shapiro, S. B. (1962). Patient wisdom: An anthology of creative insights in psychotherapy. *Journal of Psychology, 54,* 285–291.

Shaw, C. R. (1966). *The jack-roller: A delinquent boy's own story.* Chicago: University of Chicago Press. (Original work published 1930)

Shaw, C. R., & McKay, H. D. (1942). *Juvenile delinquency and urban areas: A study of rates of delinquency in relation to differential characteristics of local communities in American cities.* Chicago: University of Chicago Press.

Sheldon, W. H. (1942). *The varieties of temperament.* New York: Harper.

Sheldon, W. H. (1949). *Varieties of delinquent youth.* New York: Harper.

Shore, M. F., & Massimo, J. L. (1969). Fifteen years after treatment: A follow-up study of comprehensive vocationally-oriented psychotherapy. *American Journal of Orthopsychiatry, 49,* 240–245.

Short, J. F., & Nye, F. I. (1957). Reported behavior as a criterion of deviant behavior. *Social Problems, 5,* 207–213.

Siegel, L. J., & Senna, J. J. (1988). *Juvenile delinquency: Theory, practice, law.* St. Paul, MN: West.

Simon, W., & Gagnon, J. H. (1976). The anomie of affluence: A post-Mertonian conception. *American Journal of Sociology, 82,* 356–378.

Slack, C. W. (1960). Experimenter-subject psychotherapy: A new method of introducing intensive office treatment for unreachable cases. *Mental Hygiene, 44,* 238–256.

Slavson, S. R. (1964). *A textbook of analytic group psychotherapy.* New York: International Universities Press.

Snow, C. P. (1961). Either-or. *Progressive, 25,* 24–25.

Snyder, J. J. (1977). Reinforcement analysis of problem and non-problem families. *Journal of Abnormal Psychology, 86,* 528–535.

Snyder, J. J., & Patterson, G. (1987). Family interaction and delinquent behavior. In H. C. Quay (Ed.), *Handbook of juvenile delinquency.* New York: Wiley.

Snyder, J. J., & White, M. H. (1979). The use of cognitive self-instruction in the treatment of behaviorally disturbed adolescents. *Behavior Therapy, 10,* 227–235.

Sowles, R. C., & Gill, J. H. (1970). Institutional and community adjustment of delinquents following counseling. *Journal of Consulting and Clinical Psychology, 34,* 398–402.

Stein, N., & Bogin, D. (1978). Individual child psychotherapy. In A. P. Goldstein (Ed.), *Prescriptions for child mental health and education.* New York: Pergamon.

Stephenson, R., & Scarpitti, F. (1968). A study of probation effectiveness. *The Journal of Criminal Law, Criminology and Police Science, 59*, 361–369.

Strean, H. (1959). The use of the patient as consultant. *Psychoanalysis and Psychoanalytic Review, 45*, 36–44.

Strodtbeck, E. L., Short, J. F., & Kolegar, E. (1962). The analysis of self-descriptions by members of delinquent gangs. *Sociological Quarterly, 3*, 331–356.

Stuart, R. B., Jayaratne, S., & Tripoldi, T. (1976). Changing adolescent deviant behavior through reprogramming the behavior of parents and teachers. *Canadian Journal of Behavioral Science, 8*, 132–144.

Sutherland, E. H. (1937). *Principles of criminology* (3rd ed.). Philadelphia: Lippincott.

Sutherland, E. H. (1947). *Principles of criminology* (4th ed.). Philadelphia: Lippincott.

Sutherland, E. H., & Cressey, D. R. (1974). *Criminology.* New York: Lippincott.

Sykes, G. M., & Matza, D. (1957). Techniques of neutralization: A theory of delinquency. *American Sociological Review, 22*, 664–670.

Tannenbaum, F. (1938). *Crime and the community.* Boston: Ginn.

Tappan, P. (1960). *Crime, justice and correction.* New York: McGraw-Hill.

Taylor, T., & Watt, D. C. (1977). The relation of deviant symptoms and behaviour in a normal population to subsequent delinquency and maladjustment. *Psychological Medicine, 7*, 163–169.

Tennenbaum, D. J. (1977). Personality and criminality: A summary and implications of the literature. *Journal of Criminal Justice, 5*, 225–235.

Terrance, M. (1971). *Positive Action for Youth (PAY).* Flint, MI: Flint Board of Education, Mott Crime and Delinquency Prevention Program.

Thornton, G. (1939). The ability to judge crimes from photographs of criminals. *Journal of Abnormal and Social Psychology, 34*, 378–383.

Toch, H. (1969). *Violent men.* Chicago: Aldine.

Toruk, L. (1974). *Straight talk from prison: A convict reflects on youth, crime and society.* New York: Human Sciences.

Trasler, G. (1987). Biogenetic factors. In H. C. Quay (Ed.), *Handbook of juvenile delinquency.* New York: Wiley.

Trojanowicz, R. C., & Morash, M. (1987). *Juvenile delinquency: Concepts and control.* Englewood Cliffs, NJ: Prentice-Hall.

Tyler, V., & Brown, G. (1968). Token reinforcement of academic performance with institutionalized delinquent boys. *Journal of Educational Psychology, 59,* 164–168.

Vanden Haeg, E. (1975). *Punishing criminals: Concerning a very old and painful question.* New York: Basic.

Vorrath, H., Brendtro, L. K. (1974). *Positive peer culture.* Chicago: Aldine.

Voss, H. L. (1963). Ethnic differentials in delinquency in Honolulu. *Journal of Criminal Law, Criminology and Police Science, 54,* 322–327.

Wahler, R. G. (1980). The insular mother: Her problems in parent-child treatment. *Journal of Applied Behavior Analysis, 13,* 207–219.

Wahler, R. G., Leske, G., & Rogers, E. S. (1978). The insular family: A deviance support system for oppositional children. In L. A. Hamerlynck (Ed.), *Behavioral systems for the developmentally disabled: In school and family environments.* New York: Brunner/Mazel.

Waldo, G. P., & Dinitz, S. (1967). Personality attributes of the criminal: An analysis of research studies, 1950–65. *Journal of Research in Crime and Delinquency, 4,* 185–202.

Walter, H. I., & Gilmore, S. K. (1973). Placebo versus social learning effects in parent training procedures designed to alter the behavior of aggressive boys. *Behavior Therapy, 4,* 361–377.

Warren, M. Q. (1974). *Classification for treatment.* Paper presented at the National Institute of Law Enforcement and Criminal Justice seminar on the classification of criminal behavior, Washington, DC.

Warren, M. Q. (1983). Applications of interpersonal-maturity theory to offender populations. In W. S. Laufer & J. M. Day (Eds.), *Personality theory, moral development, and criminal behavior.* Lexington, MA: Lexington.

Wegmann, T. G., & Smith, D. W. (1963). Incidence of Klinefelter's syndrome among juvenile delinquents and felons. *Lancet, 1,* 274.

West, D. J. (1967). *The young offender.* Harmondsworth, England: Penguin.

West, D. J., & Farrington, D. P. (1977). *The delinquent way of life.* London: Heinemann.

White, G. D., Nielson, G., & Johnson, S. M. (1972). Timeout duration and the suppression of deviant behavior in children. *Journal of Applied Behavior Analysis, 5,* 111–120.

Wilkins, L. T., & Gottfredson, D. M. (1969). *Research, demonstration and social action.* Davis, CA: National Council on Crime and Delinquency.

Williams, D., & Akamatsu, J. (1978). Cognitive self-guidance training with juvenile delinquents: Applicability and generalization. *Cognitive Therapy and Research, 2,* 205–208.

Williams, T., & Kornblum, W. (1985). *Growing up poor.* Lexington, MA: Heath.

Wilson, H. (1980). Parental supervision: A neglected aspect of delinquency. *British Journal of Criminology, 20,* 203–235.

Wilson, J. Q., & Hernnstein, R. J. (1985). *Crime and human nature.* New York: Simon & Schuster.

Wiltz, N. A., & Patterson, G. R. (1974). An evaluation of parent training procedures designed to alter inappropriate aggressive behavior of boys. *Behavior Therapy, 5,* 215–221.

Witkin, H. A., Mednick, S. A., Schulsinger, F., Ballestrom, E., Christiansen, K. O., Goodenough, D. R., Hirschborn, K., Lundsteen, C., Owen, D. R., Philip, J., Rubin, D. B., & Stocking, M. (1976). Criminality, aggression and intelligence among XYY and XXY men. *Science, 193,* 547.

Wolfgang, M., Figlio, R., & Sellin, T. (1972). *Delinquency in a birth cohort.* Chicago: University of Chicago Press.

Woodson, R. O. (1981). *A summons to life: Mediating structures and prevention of youth crime.* Cambridge, MA: Ballinger.

Wright, W. E., & Dixon, M. C. (1977). Community prevention and treatment of juvenile delinquency: A review of evaluation studies. *Journal of Research in Crime and Delinquency, 14,* 35–67.

Yalom, S. D., & Elkin, G. (1974). *Every day gets a little closer: A twice-told therapy.* New York: Basic.

Yochelson, S., & Samenow, S. E. (1976). *The criminal personality.* New York: Aronson.

Author Index

Subject Index

About the Author

Arnold P. Goldstein, PhD, joined the clinical psychology section of Syracuse University's Psychology Department in 1963 and both taught there and directed its Psychotherapy Center until 1980. In 1981, he founded the Center for Research on Aggression, which he currently directs. He joined Syracuse University's Division of Special Education in 1985. Dr. Goldstein has a career-long interest, as both researcher and practitioner, in difficult-to-reach clients. Since 1980, his main research and psychoeducational focus has been incarcerated juvenile offenders and child-abusing parents. He is the developer of Structured Learning, a psychoeducational program and curriculum designed to teach prosocial behaviors to chronically antisocial persons. Dr. Goldstein's many books include, among others, *Aggression Replacement Training: A Comprehensive Intervention for Aggressive Youth; Changing the Abusive Parent; The Prepare Curriculum: Teaching Prosocial Competencies; Refusal Skills: Preventing Drug Use in Adolescence;* and *Skillstreaming the Adolescent: A Structured Learning Approach to Teaching Prosocial Skills.*